INTRODUCTION TO STILL LIFE AND FLOWER PAINTING

By the same author

BEGINNER'S GUIDE TO PAINTING IN OILS
BEGINNER'S GUIDE TO WATER COLOUR PAINTING
BEGINNER'S GUIDE TO PORTRAIT PAINTING
BEGINNER'S GUIDE TO PAINTING THE NUDE

Introduction to Still Life and Flower Painting

BARBARA DORF

PELHAM BOOKS

First published in Great Britain by Pelham Books Ltd
52 Bedford Square, London WC1B 3EF
1976

ISBN 0 7207 0885 0

Set and printed in Great Britain by
Tonbridge Printers Ltd, Peach Hall Works, Tonbridge, Kent
in Plantin eleven on twelve point on paper supplied by
P. F. Bingham Ltd, and bound by James Burn
at Esher, Surrey

Acknowledgements

The author/artist gratefully thanks and acknowledges the following: Winsor and Newton, artists' colourmen; George Rowney, artists' colourmen; Studio Vista, who have been acknowledged in the text; S.P.A.D.E.M. Marlborough Fine Art who have generously allowed me to reproduce the Jackson Pollock drawings; the Witt Library; Victoria Cooper; Anne Pennington; and my mother.

Contents

CHAPTER I

Introduction

To see a World in a grain of sand,
And a Heaven in a wild flower,
Hold Infinity in the palm of your hand,
And Eternity in an hour.

William Blake's verse from *Auguries of Innocence* is a very good way of describing still life painting. Still life paintings are about the ordinary objects of common experience, transformed by the artist's vision into paint within the confines of the picture's edges. Still life is about your painting, perhaps one painting in a whole life-time that is so ordinary and yet very special. Everyone who has ever painted has probably once achieved something of permanent value in a still life. Many of you create still lifes every day without thinking of them as such; the way you put jars on a shelf, set a table, arrange chairs to your liking. This is the beginning of still life, it is your way of doing things that is intensely individual, a result of the way your body and mind is conditioned and programmed. This instinct to arrange and place agreeably is part of the reason why we respond to all works of art and, moreover, is a conscious faculty that raises man above the dumb beasts. We can find in small galleries utterly satisfying still lifes by an otherwise unknown painter, that we feel we wish we had painted. It is true that great artists paint the still life, and often we feel we can understand their world view through a small still life better than a figure composition. In a still life you and the onlooker can distil your own universe from objects in your own painting. The universe you can create, if you consider still life paintings that you have seen, can be opulent, intimate, sensual, joyful or subdued. They can, as the name suggests, be still, but they can convey rhythm too. When the great French philosopher and encyclopaedist Diderot wrote of Chardin, 'the peaches and grapes give appetite and attract your fingers', it reminds us that still life also appeals to the sense of touch.

The still life may have existed in Roman painting. Some surviving paintings may have been painted for the artist's pleasure in the objects, or as a trick for the eye, so that the onlooker thinks he is seeing things on a shelf but it is really only a painting; these may have been trade signs. Another example of joking representation is a Roman mosaic flooring with objects that look as though they should have been swept up!

Still life did not emerge as a western art form till about 1580 or so. Flowers and fruit have been represented since the dawn of the arts of man but in most cases they have been decorative, symbolic, or both, like the lotus in Egyptian art. For us, in the latter quarter of the twentieth century, it may be hard to see that paintings and even the external world itself were seen symbolically until about 1600. Symbolic interpretation declined with the gradual decline in superstition. So, if we look at flowers and fruit in most paintings, pre- about 1580, purely as aesthetic objects in painting, it is only half understanding painting. An obvious example is the lily in an annunciation. The artist probably did respond aesthetically to the lily but the reason for it in an annunciation is because it was universally recognised as the symbol of Our Lady. The symbolism of fruit and flowers was a commonly accepted language and some of this survives today, e.g. the laurel for triumph, and the oak for fortitude; whereas the symbolism that is almost forgotten is the symbolic representation of the rhetorical gesture. Often enough you see details of flowers and fruit from paintings photographed as though they were independent of all the other parts, for example the astrolabes and music in Holbein's famous painting of *The Ambassadors* in the National Gallery. In no way was Holbein painting a still life as such. It is a double portrait and the figures stand as heraldic bearers do, each side of a still life of all the attributes of the liberal arts. Representation of the attributes of the liberal arts and the major faculties were very usual in Renaissance painting and decorative arts. Italians represented the universe in fresco grandly disdaining the intimate.

The Flemings, who developed oil painting as we know it now, represented the universe by the building up of small details and textures. Hence, it is not surprising that still life as we understand it emerged in the low countries. The first still lifes seemed to coincide with the decline in the Protestant Netherlands of commissions for directly, doctrinal religious paintings, and earliest known still lifes were painted to point a moral, rather than to teach doctrine. They contain objects that we associate with mortality and all-consuming time – a skull, an hour glass, fading leaves, etc. Another origin of the still life were pictures of Our Lady garlanded with the flowers that symbolise her joys, sorrows, etc., where the artist has clearly been more interested in the flowers. So, by about 1600, the still life developed to an art form in its own right. Once it was thought of as an independent art form, like landscape, it took the imagination of painters of every degree all over Europe till the present day. The seventeenth century was one of the great ages of every type of painting, including still life. Still lifes were painted for the artist's own satisfaction, or for the patron who wanted his priceless possessions or gorgeous tulips immortalised. The still life that was painted as a reminder of the vanity of earthly goods survived in a way, but the artist's attitude is clearly ambivalent. He has obviously thoroughly enjoyed the objects that he represents while telling a moral against them. Some of the still lifes with books in them are illustrations of the text that 'knowledge shall fail'; a caterpillar in pretty flowers was a reminder that 'the flower fadeth'. In a good still life, like a subject painting, the vision of the artist is above the incidents of narrative detail. Some still lifes were an extension of the owner's identity, his heraldic symbols.

The seventeenth century was also a time of the foundation of academies of art and the formulation of art theories. One theory that dominated academic thinking till about 1840, was the idea of hierarchy in art. The highest form of painting was the figure composition from an imposing subject like an epic poem, then descending through the nude, the portrait, the landscape, the genre and last of all a still life. While it is true that a good still life is better than a bad figure composition, the hierarchy is at any rate a gauge of difficulty. Only the very greatest painters have painted good figure compositions; yet painters of every order of magnitude have painted good still lifes. Among the greatest compositions are, say, those of Giotto in the Arena Chapel, Michelangelo's Sistine Chapel, Raphael's *School of Athens*, Velasquez *Surrender of Breda*. (If you formulate a list it will probably be quite different.) What these have in common is that they extend our experience and our interpretation of the universe. The artist's vision is larger and grander than the norm. A still life is never on the level of interpreting the nature of god or man, and we cannot expect it to. But a still life can reflect pleasingly on what we know anyway, and enjoy being reminded of. Or a still life can, at least, present a formally ordered, recreated universe of great intensity like those of Cézanne and Chardin.

The art theorists would also have dismissed the still life for its lack of intellectual content. It is true that most still lifes have been painted for pure pleasure; and rightly, Aristotle reminds us 'pleasure is a good thing'. The artist has delighted in colour, tone and texture. Plato quotes Socrates as saying, 'The true pleasures are those which arise from the colours we call beautiful and from shapes'. Many still lifes have obviously been painted spontaneously, even all in one go. Yet, some painters have used the still life to experiment deliberately in tonality, harmony, colour, rhythm and composition. Best known of these are Chardin, Cézanne and the Cubist painters, and Morandi. They have used the still life to explore the most complex problems of paintings. So you can see that the range of a still life is very great.

If you see a still life that you take to, and one is inclined to 'take to' still life, you probably get the feeling that it was painted specially for you. One can never feel this about the figure composition in the grand manner, and one was not meant to. It is curious that a still life painted at the same time as a large historical painting by Rubens or Poussin, may seem to us to be more modern. For in the historical painting, the figures from the external world are idealised and symbolised to tell a story. The objects in a still life are themselves. It is just this feeling of intimate directness that one should receive from still lifes painted by others and give in still lifes painted by you. It is very likely that the first picture you will sell will be a still life. Selling and exhibiting have a chapter to themselves.

Something about the book. It is impossible to write a detached book about the creative arts, apart from purely factual information, and what is factual to some is subjective interpretation to another. There has been some attempt at classifiying tonality and design. It is only an attempt, for unlike seventeenth-century Rome there is no entirely common language, and it is bound in the end to be personal. Classifications are like nets, one hopes they let in more than they keep out. The classifications under chapter headings are for convenience and not final definition. The assumption is that you believe, as I certainly do, that painting can be learned. When one says 'learn to be a painter', it is silly to set one's ambitions too high, though you will certainly be able to learn enough to give yourself and others a very reasonable degree of pleasure. Do not think that there is some extra dimension that makes for 'genius'. There may be, but do not rely on it, or despair if you do not think you have got it. Remember that an artist who is considered serious and competent in one generation can be hailed as a genius in the next, and this differs from person to person. Ignore the people who say they were 'self taught'. Constable's statement is worth quoting: 'A self taught person is taught by somebody very ignorant indeed.' To return to how the book is arranged. It is true that learning implies that knowledge is systematically acquired. But what is a system for painting? The book is so arranged, as far as is reasonable, that you can start at any point. In any case how many of us read books from beginning to end without looking into the middle and last pages? You can start by slowly working through drawing basic design and painting, gradually acquiring more complex skills, in a rather formal way, like learning grammar. Or else you can start at chapter 'x' by making unholy messes and deciding that, after all you should sort yourself out. Are you thumbing through the book, disappointed that there are no colour, let alone black and white photographs to look at? This is deliberate. It is arguable, but far too many artists and art students are becoming completely dependent on photographs or colour slides. Indeed, these reproductions in media are taken for the art form in themselves. Paintings for some art students have become objects that are absorbed from slides, sitting down in a dark room. Even in some cases accompanied by tapes of associative and contemporary music. But this is not really what painting is about. Of course you need reproductions to see pictures you cannot see in the original. But a reproduction of all paintings pre-1955 is only a reminder, not the art form. After 1955 art works were deliberately produced on the McCluhan principle – the medium is the message. Sadly, one even meets people who prefer photo-reproductions to the originals. The photograph can be used to distort art history. Photographic details of Old Masters' paintings are shown suggesting that they anticipate impressionism or the moderns or whatever. We must remember that until 1860 or so, the only means of picture reproduction were the various processes of engraving and sometimes only an outline drawing of an antique or a great painting inspired another artist to a great work of art. An original painting then, and you. What you should do is to go to your local museum or gallery and wander among the still life paintings. The light may be bad, noisy children around, you have leg ache, you would like a cup of coffee. Let a still life or flower painting take your attention; in Paul Klee's words, 'Let the picture look at you.' Look at the painting. Look. There it is, a still life, an oil painting, the work of somebody's eye, mind, hand and body. Now take in, without naming the objects, the shapes, tones and the paint. It may be by a minor master or anonymous. But you, yes you, are richer and increased by looking at it. This is where your work comes in. You may create a small still life that for somebody of a subsequent generation is a moment of richness and fulfilment. Rather like having a favourite hymn tune that evokes a whole world for you; your childhood, your first response to works of art. Yet the tune was written by an unknown organist lying buried:

> Far from the madding crowd's ignoble strife
> Their sober wishes never learn'd to stray;
> Along the cool sequester'd vale of life
> They kept the noiseless tenor of their way.

None of this excludes the fact that you should see the still lifes of the major masters and every other sort of painting.

This is only a beginner's guide. Rightly, most of us throw away guide books after a time and go off on our own tracks. To reject what we have learned is a positive and natural way to learn too. The still life may properly lead us to something more ambitious. It may lead us to enlarge our horizons to something quite different. Have you something or someone telling you what you should be doing is improving the world in some way? You are. Finally, major and minor painters, ordinary painters are the people who paint. You become a painter by painting. The untalented student who finishes his pictures outstrips the legendary 'genius student' who never finishes a painting. So as Zola said to Cézanne in 1860, 'You are an artist. Come then . . . Pick up your brushes and start.'

Book list		*Shelfmark*
General:	FURST, HERBERT, *The Art of Still Life Painting*, 1927	918.5 Fur.
	STERLING, CHARLES, *Still Life Painting From Antiquity to the Present Time*, 1959	918.5 Ste.
Chardin:	WILDENSTEIN, GEORGES, Paris, 1933. Faber Gallery, 1948	Fol. 922.9 Cha. W. sm. fol. 922.9 Cha.
Fantin-Latour:	*Flower Paintings* (Exhib. Cat.) London, 1962	922.9 Fan.Z.
Cézanne:	Various Large illustrations in *Novotny*, Phaidon, 1937	922.9 Cez.N.
Van Gogh:	Various Large illustrations in SCHAPIRO, MEYER, 1951,	924.9 Gog.S.
	and UHDE, WILHELM, Phaidon, 1941	924.9 Gog.U.
Matisse:	Various	922.9 Mat.
Cubism:	COOPER, DOUGLAS, *The Cubist Epoch*, Phaidon, 1971	918.4 Z.

Braque:	RUSSELL, JOHN, 1959	922.9 Bra.R.
Juan Gris:	KAHNWEILIR, S. H., 1947	923.9 Gri.K.
Derain:	SUTTON, DENYS, Phaidon, 1959	922.9 Der.S.
Magritte:	Arts Council Exhibition Catalogue, 1969	924.9 Mag.Z.
Chirico:	GAFFE, RENÉ, Brussels, 1946	921 Chi.G.
Ben Nicholson:	SUMMERSON, JOHN, 1948 Exhibition Catalogue	928.9 Nic.S. 928.9 Nic.Z.
Francis Hodgkins:	EVANS, MYFANWY, 1948	928.9 Hod.E.
Matthew Smith:	Exhibition Catalogues, 1953 and 1960	928.9 Smi.Z.
Morandi:	Arts Council Exhibition, 1870	921.9 Mor.Z.
Rauschenberg:	Prints 1948/1970 Exhibition Catalogue, 1970	U.L. 929.9 Rau.Z.

CHAPTER 2

Boards, Paints, Brushes and Media

You are a beginner to painting. You begin with a brush, board or canvas and paint. But it is not as casual as this. You have to use very good canvas, board and paint so that it is pleasing to use the materials and you will want to use your materials as well as possible. This will mean too, that even if a painting is a failure, it will at any rate be a decent bit of craftsmanship that was worth doing. Presumably it was the idea of handling the paint that made you want to begin in the first place so you should make the handling agreeable. Note, I do not say 'easy', you did not start to paint for this reason; but there is no point in overcoming useless difficulties. Working with shoddy materials will create quite unnecessary obstacles and depress you before you begin. Remember that one of the attractions of a still life can be the sheer quality of the paint itself. The sense of touch works many ways; how your sense of touch responded to what you saw, and how you respond to your paint, brush and board. Have you ever looked at paintings, and this mean *paintings*, not photo-reproductions, and enjoyed the texture for its own sake? This is what quality in painting is. Only a house painter just pastes paint on. It is not only a question of the oil paint, but what you paint on, and the nature of your brushes. This appears to be a long apologia for using excellent materials. We are fast approaching an age where for the first time in 150 years, paints and equipment will be expensive. This is no bad thing. The more expensive, the more you will respect them. The curious thing is how beginners to painting, who maybe have not been to art school need a lot of persuading to get the best materials. This never seems to apply to people taking up other hobbies. The best though does not always mean the most expensive. Here are a few things that *you can do without*: sketching easels, these always fall to bits and do not stay steady; fancy tin dippers, these are silly, so are expensive, set-out boxes of paints and brushes. Not that there is anything wrong with them if you can afford them. But this is about saving money. You can carry paints in any sort of box and brushes well wrapped up in cotton rag. But on no account can you save on board, canvas, paint or medium and brushes.

SUPPORTS

Board. I shall use this term throughout the text when I mean what you actually paint on. Even if you are actually painting on canvas remember if a support is wrong then the whole painting will be wrong too. Patent building boards are a case where modern inventions have improved on tradition, and the new method cheaper than any other. When you see in a catalogue 'painted on panel' it means wood panel. Over the years the finest wood panels have warped and cracked. But as far as reasonable tests can show building boards, which are wood fibres bonded under pressure, are as durable as anything can be. The ones to use are those that are bonded most tightly, some are loosely bonded. You should also use board that has the smoothest surface. On no account be tempted to think that the grainy surface that you see on the back of building board is like canvas; it is not. Paintings on it look quite awful. To give the smooth and sometimes shiny surface a 'tooth' go over it with sandpaper. You cannot paint on board direct, it has to be primed. This is dealt with below. In England, 'Hardwood' is the name of a very good, commonly available board, 'Sundeala' is excellent too. In the U.S.A. 'Compact' boards and 'Presdwood' are suitable for supports. All building boards must be sized and should be primed.

Plywood, metals and glass have been used as supports. Plywood warps, metal bends, glass breaks and all of them are easily spoiled. Only use these if there really is nothing else as, say, Gaugin isolated on Tahiti was obliged to.

Cardboard has been used continually in the past, but some technicians believe it grows mould if sized. At the time of writing it is no cheaper than building boards.

Canvas, that is *linen canvas.* Make quite certain that you are *not* buying cotton or jute, both of which have a very limited life. Canvas comes in various degrees from very fine to rough and coarse. Canvas must be sized and primed.

Ready-primed canvas. This is sold by some colourmen. The difficulty here is that colourmen are inclined to be coy about the content of the priming. Buying ready-primed canvas is very much easier than priming canvas yourself, and canvas primed by professionals has a much better surface.

Ready-stretched canvases. The most expensive support, but if you can afford them they are very nice.

Stretching canvas. The attraction of canvas is that it has a drum-like surface, which some painters find very responsive to the touch of the brush. The tightness is effected by stretching the canvas over mitred stretchers. Stretchers are sold separately in artists' colourmen. As canvas is subject to shrinking or loosening, mitred stretchers are desirable, so that you can tighten the canvas by knocking in pegs. Both Jackson Pollock and Bonnard have painted extensively on the canvas before stretching it.

Sizing and priming canvas. Canvas should be sized and primed after it is put on the stretcher. Raw canvas must not be stretched too tightly. After sizing, canvas will go disconcertingly taut, but will slacken a bit later.

PRIMERS OR GROUNDS

You *cannot* paint with oil directly on to supports. If you do, the oil will sink in, separating from the pigment and the paint will crack and fall off. The oil will also rot any organic support. So you are obliged to isolate the support in some way from the paint. Here below is how.

Acrylic grounds. The most up-to-date primer sold by most art stores. It can be put straight on to the support as it contains no oil. It is very convenient as it dries within a matter of hours and is constantly used in art schools. When you use it, paint the first coat on diluted with water to the consistency of single cream. Paint on in large criss-cross strokes. Leave about one hour. Paint on the second coat to the consistency of double cream. The best ground for cardboard. *All* other grounds contain *oil,* therefore, on *no account* should they be applied to a support directly, or the support and ground will separate. To prevent this, the support *must* be sized.

Size. Thin glue that is impervious to oil. All technical experts agree that:

Rabbit skin glue has never been improved on, neither has the recipe for making it up. You should have:
1 part (*weight*) rabbit glue to 15 parts water. Soften the glue in cold water, then heat in a double saucepan. *Never boil*. When the mixture has cooled a bit, but not gone solid, paint one coat on the support and let it dry for three days or even longer.

Grounds that contain oil. Most artists' colourmen make ready-made, oil-based priming. The best priming is . . .

White lead in linseed oil which is very poisonous and slow drying. It should be thinned with turpentine. A traditional ground that has a very attractive surface to paint on, rather soft and warm.

Other oil primers. Do not be tempted to buy cheap ones from house decorators. Some colourmen sell special oil primers. Unless it specifically states that it is white lead, it is most likely to be titanium white bound in a quick drying resin. Inclined to be a bit shiny and glossy on hardboard. Good on canvas.

Emulsion priming. A very brilliant white emulsion ground, dries matt. Do not be tempted, unless it is desperate, to use house-painters' emulsion as a ground. This priming is very slightly better for boards than for canvas. You should break one egg into a screw-top jar, add an equal quantity of linseed oil and twice as much again of water. With a palette knife add to titanium white powder to form a stiff paste. Thin to the correct consistency with already prepared size.

Putting grounds on supports. After size has dried put the first coat on with a decorators' brush in large, square, even strokes with the ground to the consistency of single cream. Leave to dry; the first coat of lead ground should be left about five days. Then apply the next coat which should be the consistency of double cream. Two coats are right, more coats are an agreeable luxury. After applying the second coat *you must* let white lead grounds dry for about three weeks or longer before using.

Supports. It is much more economical and efficient, of course, to prepare a whole lot in advance.

Painting boards. Prepared by most artists' colourmen. The best are boards actually covered with fine canvas. The cheaper type are covered with a specially prepared paper embossed to imitate canvas. It is a bad imitation. Prepared painting boards are not cheap; prepare your own.

COLOUR

This means for you, as an artist, the oil paints that you will squeeze from a tube on to a palette. Today, when there are many books on colour theory on the market, all beautifully produced and printed, it is all too easy to get carried away by ideas that do not have much to do with the character of oil paint. This is not to condemn colour theories out of hand or anything else that inspires your work, but your main job is to paint and not let theory, or anything else, distract you. But as the most distracting thing to a beginner is not being in control of your equipment, the main emphasis will be on this.

Colour theories should not be dismissed altogether, so here is a word about them. They divide into three types:

Firstly, colour to express emotion. In paintings by western European masters up to about 1660, there was a generally accepted language of the symbolism of colour derived from liturgical use. Some of this is still reasonably valid today; blue being heavenly, purple for splendour and solemnity. In eighteenth-century England transparent brown varnish bitumen was used in painting because it made pictures rich and dark like those of Carracci and Titian. Brown, therefore, equalled solemnity. Time has shown that bitumen, in fact, darkens and cracks and should never be used in oil painting. Yet you only have to think of that master of the modern still life, Georges Braque, who made brown convey a light-hearted mood. Gaugin believed that colour could inspire the same basic feelings as music. Van Gogh once said he would use 'red and green, the terrible colours of men's passions'. In the distant past the liturgical colours would have been read as they were for the emotions they conveyed. Today it is much more a matter of how the beholder is personally affected. But there is one aspect of the 'mood' of colours that is very important and turns up in many handbooks. This is the expression *hot* and *cold* colours, implying that when we look at some we feel hot or cold. It is quite obvious, red and orange based colours are 'warm', and blue to blacks are 'cold'. It is a convenient generalisation, but do not forget the beautiful cold reds and browns of Velasquez and Monet's warm blue seas. Then there is the theory of colours as the components of white light. Since the seventeenth century it has been known that white light basically consists of three complementary colours; green-yellow, blue and red. By mixing these colours you obtained others:

(a)		(b)	(c)
Red+yellow	=	Orange	Blue left out
Red+blue	=	Purple	Yellow left out
Blue+yellow	=	Green	Red left out

The colours in column (b) and column (c) complement each other. The later impressionists, and especially Seurat, used this as the basis of an extensive technique and it will be discussed in greater detail in Chapter 11. Finally, theory or no, a painting is about oil paint.

OIL PAINT

Pigment suspended in linseed oil. The idea of suspending pigment in oil was known in Roman times and probably earlier. It seems to have been used throughout the Middle Ages. There are accounts for linseed oil to be used with pigment in Westminster Abbey, London. Oil and pigment may have been for preservation purposes. The legend that the technique was 'invented' by the Van Eycks in Flanders, was an Italian legend recorded by Vasari in his *Lives of Artists*. The legend contains a fair grain of truth. For, what obviously happened is that the Van Eycks, especially Jan, simplified, perfected and saw the full use of oil paint. By the beginning of the seventeenth century oil paint was used more commonly than any other media because of its range and versatility. Huge mounted oil paintings even began to supersede fresco in popularity. In oil painting you can see the quality of the artist's handling of the paint. In two more or less contemporary still lifes, Rembrandt's *Flayed Ox* and Claez *Glass and Lemon*, this is very obvious, and as much what the painting is about as the subject. In fresco painting this kind of quality does not occur. You find very little of it in the new:

Acrylic polymer colours. These comparatively new colours are lively, durable, useful. But there is a similarity in texture in all the colours, and in density too. They have made it possible over the last twenty years for artists to paint large, cheerful pictures, both abstract and figurative, pop paintings. Much of the beautiful, contemporary applied arts in furnishings, etc., owe a lot to these paintings, some of them being much better than the pictures that inspired them. But against this, acrylic is insensitive, and lacks refinement. It is not cheaper than oil paint. I suggest that you use oil paint. Remember it is the merest edge of refinement that raises an ordinary work of art to a great one.

Until about 1770 or so, artists ground their own colours. This means grinding the dry pigment until it is really fine, and finally grinding into linseed oil. You cannot get the same effect by mixing dry pigment with linseed oil without grinding first. Grinding is laborious. The advantage of grinding your own paints is that you are absolutely certain what goes into them. The disadvantage is that some pigments lose their colour if ground too much (a piece of red glass looks pale pink when crushed). Another disadvantage is that your time is valuable and it is only good sense to let a machine do the rough work and you do the work that no machine could ever do. Nowhere in this book are traditional methods recommended if modern ones are any improvement. Regarding the manufacture of oil paint, it may be a question of grinding an oxide of a metal or natural earth into exact proportions. Some colours are liquid dyes. This has always been so, when you think of fabric dyes and the liquid colours that were used for tinting book illuminations. Liquid dyes cannot be ground in oil as such, they have to be precipitated on to alumina, then filtered to form a dry powder. Liquid dyes in the past used to be obtained from vegetable substances like madder, saffron and indigo, and from the cochineal insect, like carmine. Nowadays liquid dyes are chemical products and, unlike their vegetable predecessors, are a great improvement as regards permanence and intensity. Tradition, in this case, is worth discarding. In many cases indeed, modern methods are an improvement. Paint manufacturers have specially controlled grinding machinery which they employ after the most careful sorting and washing of the dry powdered colour. In manufactured colours the colour is ground in linseed oil or safflower oil. Then there are additives; annoyingly enough some colourmen are secretive about additives, but the usual is aluminium stearate. This stablises the colour and stops it becoming brittle. Large and reputable artists' colourmen employ chemists trained in research on pigments and media. The prime aim of their research is permanence. The sign of reputable artists' colourmen is that they not only publish the contents of their colours, but also allow members of the public to visit their factories. This is something that every painter should try to do at some time.

Listed below is a comprehensive list of colours in general use in western Europe and U.S.A., all of them permanent as far as is reasonably ascertainable. Always look at a colourman's catalogue to check that a colour is not only permanent but can be mixed safely with others. Impermanent colours are still manufactured. Nowadays it is not that these will harm other colours, but that they lose their character on mixing. But remember, when regarding colour, media and grounds, we can never be 100 per cent certain, only reasonably certain; there will always be the slight element of doubt.

Oil paint – Some general observations. Most artists' colourmen sell oil paint in two grades – the *artists' colours* and *student colours*. Student colours are for people who want to save money; they are coarser ground and instead of expensive colours being used, dyes are used that imitate these colours. Student colours are permanent, but they lack the refinement of quality. If asked, I would advise you to start off with the best. Secondly, most colours tend to be transparent and some are entirely transparent. A commonly held notion about oil paint is that it is sticky and opaque. It *can* be, but it can equally be transparent and should be used in both ways. Naturally, artists' materials have their limitations, but the pleasure of using them is because of this. Oil paint will only become really opaque when you add:

WHITE

The most important colour on your palette. The lightener of all oil colour, and yet the pigment that makes all colours opaque. Naturally, it is the lightest colour on the palette and the tonality of all the others is set by white. The brightest white in nature has to have its equivalent in white on your palette. Later on there is an exercise to find out about using almost only white. There are three whites in general use. All are the best in quality.

It is a question of preferences. Many painters have them all and use all three and there is no reason why you should not. But you cannot do without white. If you do not accept this, try to oil paint without it!

Flake white. Pure basic carbonate white lead. *Very poisonous.* Low in oil. A white pigment in use since Roman times and still the most popular. Flake white tends to be a warm colour. Its texture is thick and sticky, but once it is diluted it is semi-opaque. It makes most beautiful scumble. If it is scumbled over red, brown or orange you get very beautiful greys. Flake white is the example of the earlier comment that oil paint is transparent, as well as thick and sticky. Flake white is the most popular white, and should be used if you like pasting on paint and where you intend to build up layers. A flexible pigment and most suitable for grounds.

Zinc white. Pure zinc oxide, low in oil. A silvery, pleasant white with not a very strong character, but still agreeable to use. Lightens colours and gives them body without being too self assertive. A neutral white neither tending to warm nor cold.

Titanium white. Titanium oxide and barium sulphate. Medium in oil content. The newest discovery in whites. A very brilliant cold white. Very beautiful for pure whites. It can totally cover anything underneath it, even in a scumble. Titanium white is powdery in texture and is not really suitable for building up thick masses. Many artists, especially in the U.S.A. and Germany, temper the extremes of either titanium or flake white by mixing them with zinc white.

EARTH COLOURS

The earth colours, as they are traditionally called, have their base in natural earths found in deposits. They have been used since man started to paint. These simple colours go well together and it is possible, as a later exercise will show you, to paint pictures using these and no other colours. Apart from ancient painters, some modern painters, particularly the cubists, have used these and no other colours. Hence, in general, earth colours are indispensable.

Yellow ochre. Natural earth. Silica and clay stained by an iron oxide. Medium oil content. The lightest tone of all the earth colours. A very good mixer with all colours, makes beautiful golds when mixed with whites; makes dull greens when mixed with blues. Opaque, indispensable.

Light red. Calcined yellow ochre, opaque. Medium oil content. A hot, brick red. Mixes with blues to very attractive greys. Indispensable.

Iron oxide red (or Indian red). Ferric oxide. Sometimes brick red veering to maroon; semi-opaque. Called Sinopia in the ancient treatises on painting. Iron oxide red has been known since before writing itself. But for the beginner it is very hot, strong and pungent and it is best to stick to light red.

Raw umber. Iron oxide, silica, alumina and manganese dioxide. Medium oil content. Semi-transparent. Of all the earth colours it is the only cool colour, and for this reason very useful. Veers to green as it is, but mixed with white has a hint of violet. Indispensable.

Burnt umber. Raw umber roasted. Medium oil content. A rich, hot brown.

Raw sienna. Hydrated ferric oxide with alumina and silica. Deeper medium oil content, more transparent and more pungent than yellow ochre. Could be difficult for a beginner. Mixed with blues makes unusual greens; but in general this colour is not a sympathetic mixer.

Burnt sienna. Calcined raw sienna. Medium oil content. A very hot colour and a bad mixer, best avoided by beginners.

BLACK

All blacks, contemporary and ancient, are carbon based. Black, the darkest of all colours on the palette, is the standard by which we assess the depth of tone of all other colours, like ivory black, bone black, lamp black. The oil content is very high. This means that any area of black on a painting will dry in a very lustreless way unless you use some varnish in the painting. Black, if not neutral, alone it is warmish, but it makes mixtures very cold in character, especially with white. Many modern figurative painters do not use black. As a beginner, I suggest you use it with caution.

YELLOWS

There are many on the colourman's list and all the very best ones have only been in use in modern times. Do not use chrome yellow for fine art purposes. The beautiful Aureolin you see in colourmen's lists is sadly not permanent. All yellows are semi-opaque. Yellow is, in physics, a primary colour. Traditionally associated with gold, authority or glory.

Lemon yellow. Barium chromate or strontium chromate. Medium oil content. The lightest colour on the palette. Very brilliant, cold; all other yellows can be mixed from it. A touch of red will make lemon yellow go to mid-yellows. Lemon yellow is the nearest you can get to the primary yellow in light. Mixes with purples and blues to most unusual greens. Indispensable.

Cadmium lemon. Cadmium sulphide. Medium oil content. An expensive way of having a lemon yellow on your palette, but very nice.

Lemon yellow (synthetic). Some artists' colourmen now manufacture a lemon yellow which is an organic dye precipitated on to alumina. Once you have made sure it is permanent it is cheaper and a very good alternative to those cited above.

Cadmium yellow. Medium oil content. A most beautiful and expensive mid-yellow. The tactile quality of all cadmiums is a delight.

Mid-yellows. Most colourmen make mid-yellows that are organic pigments precipitated on to an alumina base. They sometimes carry the maker's name, like 'Winsor' or 'Rowney'. In all cases look out for the permanence.

ORANGE

You cannot mix satisfactory orange colours; and why should you, for the ready-made colour is very beautiful. Especially in physics, orange is a secondary colour.

Cadmium orange. Cadmium sulphide. Medium oil content, semi-opaque. It is worth spending money on this beautiful colour. A little goes a long way so you can afford it. Dye oranges are not so good.

REDS

Traditionally associated with blood, glory, sacrifice. In physics a primary colour. One red, at least, is indispensable.

Cadmium scarlet. Cadmium sulpho-selenide. Medium oil content. Semi-opaque. A brilliant and warm red. Expensive but goes a long way.

Cadmium red. The same content. Slightly deeper than above, a very pure and excellent red, a bit colder.

Mid-reds. Here again most colourmen manufacture an organic dye equivalent. But in the case of reds they lose their character on dilution or mixture. Use a cadmium, they are the best.

Alizarin crimson. Transparent. From medieval times this sort of colour has been used by artists. Some sort of dark red is indispensable and alizarin crimson is quite the most popular. A warm colour that has the faintest hint of brown.

Rose doré. Alizarin precipitated on to alumina. A very transparent, pale reddish pink. Will get completely lost in mixtures, but for painting flowers is useful for glazing.

Rose quinacridone. A new completely permanent organic dye colour, a cold colour. Very useful for painting flowers as it mixes to pretty pinks and glazes nicely. The colour of Rose Centifolia.

PURPLES

Only in recent times has a good purple pigment been developed. In olden times carmines were glazed into blues. Sometimes these have faded, as you can see in old pictures where there is a streaky blue or pink. Later in the nineteenth century purples were obtained by mixing crimson and ultramarine. This gives a rich dark mauve, agreeable in itself, but for a really true colour use a purple from the tube.

Pthalocyanine violet. An organic dye of that name precipitated on to alumina. Medium oil content. Transparent. Invented in 1936. A very dark, cold violet. Unusual and useful in mixtures, but for a beginner it could be troublesome. Mixed with white makes a very cold, harsh pale mauve.

Quinacridone violets. Organic dyes, coming in a variety of shades from violets to cold dark reds. Transparent, very pretty for flowers. Some are exactly the colour of Rose Cardinal Richelieu.

Mineral or manganese violet. Manganese ammonium pyrophosphate. A mid-toned violet, medium oil content, semi-opaque; a very beautiful and very expensive colour, warmer than the other violets, and keeps its warmth in mixing with white. If you cannot face the price of the mineral violet, the quinacridone violets are an excellent alternative.

Cobalt Violet. Cobalt phosphate. High in oil content. Opaque. Very light tones, grainy in mixture.

BLUE

This primary colour is, in many cultures, symbolic of heaven and eternity. At one time the finest blue was real ultramarine and this was the artists' most expensive colour. In the nineteenth century, synthetic ultramarine was discovered and also cobalt and prussian blue.

Ultramarine (artificial). Synthetic version of the costly lapis lazuli blue that was so highly prized in olden times. Soda, silicate, alumina and sulphur. Semi-opaque; medium oil content. The nearest you can get to primary blue, and the standard for all others; indispensable.

Cobalt blue. Cobalt aluminate. High oil content; opaque. A mild blue, very bright but a good mixer.

Cerulean. Cobalt stannate. Opaque, high oil content. The nearest in oil paint to turquoise. A good and useful mixer, very light toned.

Pthalocyanine blue. Organic dye on an alumina base. Transparent, dark, slightly greenish. Should be used instead of prussian blue.

GREENS

The colours of nature and spring. If you are painting flowers or plants you will certainly need one or two greens. Every green that is listed is cold. They can all be made warmer by adding any sort of yellow, red or brown. Many pretty greens are manufactured that are pleasing to look at but impermanent; do not buy them.

Viridian. Transparent hydrous oxide of chromium. Very high oil content. A cold green that mixes very well with all colours. Indispensable.

Emerald green. Synthetic organic dye on alumina. Not to be confused with the old-fashioned arsenic green which was, of course, highly poisonous. This colour is very bright, the lightest green and pleasing.

Pthalocyanine green. Sometimes marketed under the colourman's name, 'thalo' or 'monestial'. An organic dye on an alumina base. Very deep. Transparent. A very pungent colour that is best avoided until you are more experienced.

Other greens. Different colourmen sell very attractive organic dye colours that are permanent, but sold under a variety of names.

PALETTES

These are what you put the colours out on and on which you mix them. While it might set you feeling fine to have the traditional artists' mahogany palette, these are expensive and not essential. The only essential point about a palette is that it is not absorbent; so it can be laminate, glass or ceramic. If it is desperate, or you are travelling, you can use non-absorbent kitchen paper.

Palette knives. Flexible, tempered steel knives that are used to clean your palette and as you will see later, to paint with. You cannot do without one.

Painting knives. Tempered, flexible knives for painting, but too feeble for cleaning the palette. They are expensive. You can easily do without them, but by all means indulge yourself if the idea appeals to you.

BRUSHES

You cannot get started without these! Always buy the best, or always *enjoy* buying the best, not only by looking at them but by feeling the heads of the brushes. The hairs of a fine paint-brush should spring back into shape. The springiness of a paint brush is what gives it response to your handling.

Hog hair brushes are white, crisp, springy. They are used for large areas of painting. Hog hair brushes can be used to manipulate paint as they leave the imprint of the artist's handwork in the paint. This is a very personal aspect of painting as many very great painters have quite inconspicuous brushwork, while with other painters one of the aesthetic delights of their work is the handling of the paint.

Sable brushes. These leave no imprint in the paint. They are very sleek and springy and lay paint on very smoothly. Sable brushes are, and always have been, very expensive. These brushes are a delight to use and always worth getting.

Kolinsky brushes. Many a brush manufacturer sells kolinsky as sable, or names brushes 'kolinsky-sable', but there is a difference. Kolinsky is almost as good as sable but not quite. If there is a choice take sable. Though the way things are going sable brushes are fast becoming unobtainable.

Ox, marten, badger brushes. These are cheaper hairs; they have the characteristics of cheap brushes in that they do not spring back into shape easily. They are mostly used in schools. Artists should use them only for varnishing pictures.

Rags. Cotton or linen. These are for wiping brushes, your palette and even sometimes the paint surface. Synthetic fibres are worse than useless.

MEDIA

It is possible to work with paint directly from the tube and you have to if you are using only a palette knife. But more usually, and certainly in terms of permanence, to manipulate paint you should use medium, or a 'vehicle' as it is sometimes called. This is another area where beginners can get into hopeless and unnecessary muddles by thinking that this involves complicated mixing, reminiscent of an alchemist of old. The whole idea of medium is to make it easier for you to paint in the way you want to. 'Vehicle' is a good word, for the medium indeed, makes the paint 'go'. The simplest, best and most usual medium to make paint 'go' is . . .

Turpentine and linseed oil. One part of linseed oil to two parts of turpentine. Turpentine means genuine gum turpentine, sold for artists, and must never be confused with *White spirit,* sometimes sold as turps substitute. Only useful for rinsing brushes, not as a painting medium. For that matter, you should *not* use the ordinary grade linseed oil sold in oil shops. Use only the finest type sold in artists' colourmen.

Turpentine and stand oil. A *glossy* medium that does not dry too quickly, one to use if you find you like working into wet paint but leaving no brush marks. Two parts genuine turpentine and one part of stand oil. These two are enough to get a beginner started and media that are more difficult to handle will be dealt with in a later chapter.

Synthetic media. Most artists' colourmen now manufacture synthetic gels and other oil painting media. One type of synthetic gel is thixotropic and comes in a tube. It squeezes out solid, and thins by working it with a brush. It is very convenient to take on holiday as it dries quickly. As far as one can tell it is permanent. The only disconcerting thing is that it dries very glossy, but if you like this, so much the better.

BUYING FOR A BEGINNER

As a beginner, to set yourself up in equipment, here is a list of what you should get. It is much more economical to buy most equipment all at once and replace or increase when necessary, rather than buy in bits and pieces. I am assuming that most readers *want* to save money. Indeed, those who do *not* are objects of pity as they are much less likely to respect the materials they have.

Basics. You *cannot* start without the following: A piece of laminate for a palette (you can often find very nice pieces on builders' skips). A large bottle of genuine turpentine, a smaller bottle of linseed oil. Two sable brushes, one long and thin, the other square. Seven hog hair brushes of a variety of sizes and shapes, the largest about one inch across. Two clean tins, one for mixing media, the other for rinsing brushes. Rags. One very large tube of white, large tubes of raw umber, yellow ochre and light red. Medium tubes of lemon yellow, crimson, ultramarine and viridian. Prepare about twelve painting boards, one about 20 x 25 cm, another 25 x 30 cm, and the other smaller.

A fair start. You can start comfortably with the following: The above list, plus ten more hog brushes. A medium tube of cadmium red, orange, purple and cerulean. Six more prepared boards.

A stylish start. An easel, twenty more brushes, plus the above two lists.

A luxurious start. Means the above three lists, ready made-up canvas, as many brushes as you like, and all the gadgets and colours that take your fancy in the art shop.

CARE OF EQUIPMENT

This is one of the prime rules in painting; the care that is the expression of love of your materials. If you do not take pleasure in washing your brushes and cleaning your palette, as much as in painting itself, then it is doubtful if you are serious. In any case, care of your equipment is your greatest economy. I have, myself, sable brushes, admittedly a bit shabby now, which is not surprising as they are 100 years old! It will also set you off to a bad start if, at every painting session, your equipment is messy after the previous one.

Washing brushes. Your precious brushes, which are expensive and going to become more so, require the greatest care. If caring for equipment is going to be a bore, then sorry – but painting isn't for you.

1. Rinse brushes well in turpentine.
2. Wipe as clean as possible on cotton rag.
3. Rinse brushes under cold water.
4. Rub on to a cake of kitchen soap – the finest toilet soap is no better.
5. Rub the brushes into the palms of your hands till more dirt comes out.
6. Repeat stages 3, 4 and 5, till rubbing on the soap produces a thick white lather, it won't at first, but go on until it does.
7. Rinse very well under cold water. Never use hot water, it expands the metal part of the brush and eventually shortens the brushes' life.
8. Press brushes into shape, at the same time pressing out the superfluous water.
9. Leave brushes upright to dry, allow 24 hours and no less, or they will not hold the paint.

SETTING OUT A PALETTE

Setting out a palette is one of the disciplines of the painter's art that helps the artist get into an organised frame of mind before beginning to paint. The idea is to have a system and then to stick to it. These are the usual schemes for setting out a palette. The first is to line up the colours in the order of the spectrum: yellows, reds, violets, blues, greens, browns and earths, and black and white at the end. The other is to line up, on opposite sides of the palette, the cold and warm colours. You should also have two separate containers, one for your media, and another larger container with turpentine to rinse your brushes. On no account mix these. You can see in artists' colourmen rather natty little containers made specially to carry media. Have them if money is no object, but otherwise empty tins and glass jars are just as good.

Some other books. There is Gettens and Stout's *Painting Materials, a Short Encyclopaedia,* published very usefully in Dover paperbacks. Then there are the many books by Ralph Mayer on the materials of the artist, which well repay study. Ralph Mayer also writes for that excellent journal, *American Artist,* which has very good articles on up-to-date techniques.

SOME DEFINITIONS

Throughout the text there will be various terms that are continually used and before we begin these should be defined, just in case there is somebody saying, 'depends on what you mean by' . . .

Warm colours. The colours that are in the red-orange range. They are the colours of fire and make us think of heat and warmth.

Cold colours. Colours in the blue-black range, colours of deep water and night. Blue is the traditional colour of heaven and remoteness.

The following definitions, taken from the *Shorter Oxford English Dictionary,* are reproduced by kind permission of the Oxford University Press:

Composition. The action or art of disposing the parts of a work of art, so as to form a harmonious whole.

Form. The visible aspect of a thing; . . . configuration.

Line. A continuous extent (whether straight or curved) of length without breadth or thickness; the limit of a surface.

Surface. The outermost part of a material body, considered with respect to its form, texture, or extent.

CHAPTER 3

How to Draw for a Still Life

How to draw? How do you imagine you should draw? Most probably your first instinct is the correct one. Put a line round something and there you are, you have form. Put a line round what? The title is still life, so we will not depart from that. A cylinder, a sphere (toy ones with lines round are very good), a cube and a rectangular box on the table, and there you are – a still life. If you really are a beginner, before you begin let us consider what you draw with and on what. You cannot begin too soon to be concerned about every aspect of your equipment. One hears the annoying commonplace 'a bad workman blames his tools'. More accurately, a bad workman will not care enough about his work to get good ones. With poor tools and materials you get depressed before you start.

DRAWING MEDIA

Pencils are a comparatively recent invention. Everyone knows about them, or do they? We have all used them almost without thinking. But now we ought to think about using quality artists' pencils which are made of the best graphite. They range from very hard to very soft. The hardest pencils soon wear down the surface of the paper. Pencils, of all the drawing media in common use, are the least attractive in themselves. Ink and charcoal are pleasing and the fact that pencils are not means that it is less easy to disguise your mistakes. Mannerisms and weaknesses show up alarmingly in pencil. Pencil can be rubbed out, but this is not an advantage. On the contrary, relying on rubbing out makes for messy work and weak drawing. Try and do without a rubber. This is why many art teachers recommend . . .

Ink. Because you cannot rub this out you are obliged to draw with a sure line. Nowadays some excellent drawing inks are manufactured which have more flow than the traditional Indian ink. Indian ink has a high shellac content and dries very quickly, often clogging the pen nib.

Pens for ink. There is nothing to beat old-fashioned steel nibs and quill and reed pens. Tradition is not advised here, or indeed in any other part of the book, for the sake of it, but only when it is best. You can cut reed pens and quills yourself, but it needs some practice. Otherwise you can draw with a paint-brush in ink; diluting drawing ink with water to get half-tones. Indian ink can dissolve in water but the effect is grainy and not pleasant. I have not recommended biro or felt pens; they do not respond well to sensitive work.

Charcoal and chalks. Traditional media that have not been improved upon. Charcoal smudges easily; it is possible to overcome this by spraying the drawing with a fixative. Some artists believe that fixative, which is shellac dissolved in alcohol, spoils the surface of a charcoal drawing and as one of the attractions of charcoal is a crumbly surface, I am inclined to agree with this. The best solution to charcoal smudging is putting the drawing behind glass, so if you do a drawing that you are really pleased with, you should frame it. The foregoing applies to chalk too.

PAPER

You cannot be indifferent to paper as poor quality paper can set your drawing wrong before you start.

Quality papers are made of cotton fibres. This sort of paper is often made by hand. Cotton fibres are dissolved in vats of water. Frames crossed by wires are dipped into the vats to collect the fibres. The thicker the paper is to be, naturally, the more fibres have to be collected in the frame. The water drains out and the paper is dried between felts. It is then like blotting paper. To make the paper non-absorbent it has to be sized. The tendency of paper is to have a rough surface. Smooth surfaces are made by pressing the paper between rollers. Rough papers have a surface that takes the pattern of the wires on the frame. The traditional frames give a 'laid' or 'wove' pattern. The process described above can be done by machine. Providing the fibre is cotton these types of paper count as quality papers. It is the cotton (or linen as it sometimes is) that gives the paper its quality. Many quality papers, like 'Ingres' or 'Tumba', are tinted, often in beautiful colours. To achieve this the solution of cotton and water in the vat is dyed.

Use quality papers for water colour, also for important drawings. Use quality papers all the time if you can afford them. They are always expensive. If you find a type you like invest in getting a large quantity. At the moment of writing supplies are getting unpredictable.

Ordinary papers, most paper in everyday use for books, sketch books, newspapers; the paper that is sold as cartridge and is made of wood chips. This method was only discovered in the latter part of last century. This greatly enlarged our source of raw material for paper, and the advances in paper technology come from this. The slight disadvantage of cartridge paper as against quality paper is that it is more brittle and inclined to go yellow in the course of time. Very cheap papers are made by recycling waste paper. Cartridge papers lose their surface most disagreeably if you rub out too much. All papers that you see in artists' colourmens either loose or in sketch books are wood pulp based unless otherwise stated.

Use ordinary papers for everyday drawing and sketching, as they are considerably less expensive than quality papers.

Be careful of using some of the coloured papers like sugar packet paper, fluorescent papers and wrapping papers. These are dyed with cheap colours and fade in a matter of weeks. Be careful, too, about using papers that have a brilliant white shiny surface. These go yellow in no time.

Rubbers. Try not to use at all! But if you must, use art rubbers, the ones that are like putty. Only rub out after you have corrected your drawing. New bread is very useful for rubbing out too.

Now it is up to you to experiment with every type of drawing material.

DRAWING

To go back to where we began. We have a cube, a rectangular box, a sphere, a cylinder. Cézanne, writing in 1904 to Emile Bernard, said: 'Nature after the sphere, the cylinder and the cone.' This remark has led to every sort of interpretation; the interpretations being as interesting as the original remark. Some art historians believe that Cézanne was looking forward to the austere concepts of cubism, and twentieth-century architecture and design. Others believe that Cézanne was affirming his belief in the classical art-school training when students had to draw the geometric regular solids. Both these interpretations may be true. But why did students have to draw these solids? Part of the explanation may be that through Plato and the classical tradition they have come to be thought of as symbols of perfection, and even of divine origin. In the distant past it was usual to think that anything that had always existed was of divine origin. The circle, like a straight line, can be made with a piece of string and a peg. So with very simple tools your hand and arm can make these shapes. The peg and string make better circles and lines than your hand with pencil can, but go on and keep trying. There is a more practical explanation and this you will discover when you begin . . .

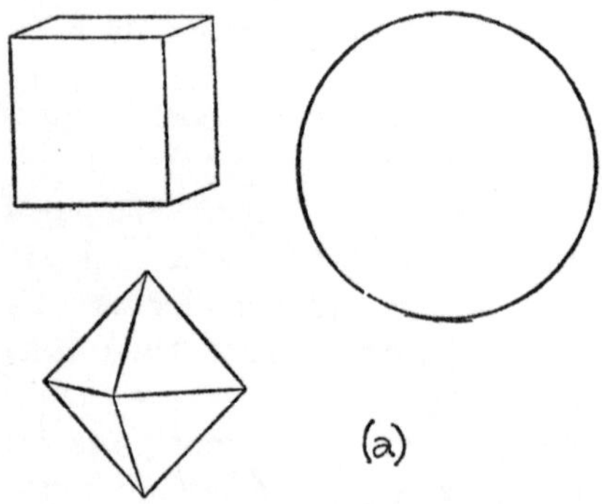

FIG. 1 (a) *The regular solids drawn with instruments are easy.* (b) *The regular solids are not at all easy to draw freehand. That's why we keep trying!*

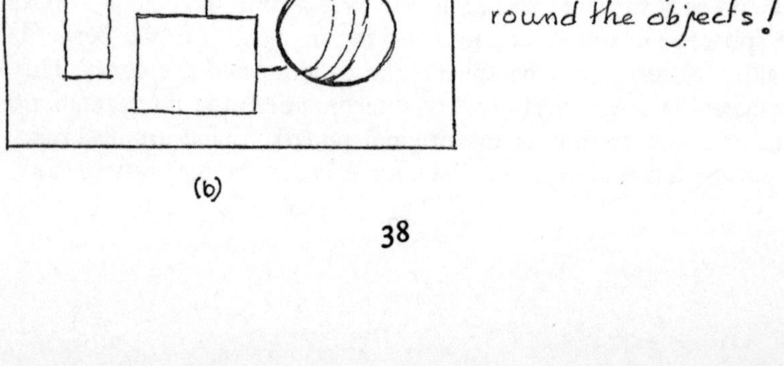

To start outline drawing. Supposing you sat down and you put the objects you are drawing in front of you, on a box, say, at eye-level. Like in the drawing Fig. 1(b) where you see everything is flat. Now if you start to draw you will see why students were set this as a basic test. All you should do at the moment is to copy the objects by a simple outline, but you will probably find that your outline is not simple and falls very short of the originals. Not only will yours fall short, but mine and everybody else's. Without compasses, rulers and angles no one can draw perfect shapes; all we can get is near approximations. So this is why this is a very valuable test of training your hand. You will get nothing out of any sort of drawing if, whenever lines go crooked, you tell yourself, 'It's meant to be like that'. Has the drawing gone wrong? Probably it has. Try another. It may be that your hand, as a beginner, cannot obey your mind. For that matter, your drawing may be going reasonably well but you still have to go on trying, keeping your outlines clear. As you go you should try to work in bold lines with the pencil. But if your hand refuses to obey your mind, it might be an idea to try some exercises to practise manual dexterity, like you do when you start to learn to write. In many cultures drawing and writing go together.

Practising lines. With bold free strokes using pen, pencil or anything else you like, copy the lines you see in Fig. 2. You

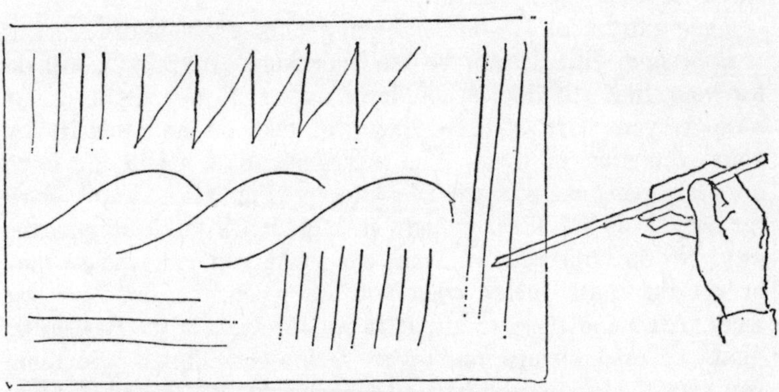

FIG. 2 *Here are exercises for manual dexterity. Practise them small and large, drawing with your arm rather than your wrist. To learn breadth of drawing, try drawing holding your pencil or pen at the far end.*

should copy them both large and small. For this sort of exercise it really does not matter what sort of paper you use, even old newspapers will do. This may seem too elementary, but the idea of lines being expressive has been fundamental to many modern painters. Here is a quotation that Seurat and his disciples admired. It is from Charles Blanc's *Grammar of the Art of Drawing,* Paris 1887.

> 'Straight, curved, horizontal or vertical, parallel or diverging, all lines have a secret relationship with feeling. In the sight of the world, as in the human figure and in architecture, straight lines correspond to a feeling of austerity and strength and repeated in a composition give the appearance of the grave, the imposing, the rigid. Horizontals express in nature the calm of the sea.'

To return to . . .

The regular solids. To draw these in simple outline is part of your basic grammar as an artist. Painting is a language, and grammar is the foundation of language. Never be timid, it is better to make a bold mistake. If things look out of proportion in relation to one another, try measuring. How lines relate one to another is what drawing is about. Try another and another. Stick to an outline, not only is it instinctive, but there is no mistake you can hide. Remember, as you would driving a car, care is about decisive action.

Take a different position and you get the problem of . . .

Extension. But do not be too ambitious. Any object will do for your first still life, a couple of apples, a jug, anything. As soon as you start to draw they will take on an intensity by your recreation of them. The arrangement of a still life is so intensely personal that the illustrations (Fig. 3(a)) simply show the way *I* do it. This, though, is a guide. A guide directs the way. No one but you, yourself, can make you take the journey or get the most out of what you see when you do. Now for work. After the plain solids, it is not too bad, is it? Earlier we discussed relationships, one object to another. This is something you should look for the whole time – height, width and distance between objects. It is a useful idea to use something in the still life as the norm to refer everything else to (see Fig. 4). Do not settle for only one view point; move around and see unexpected

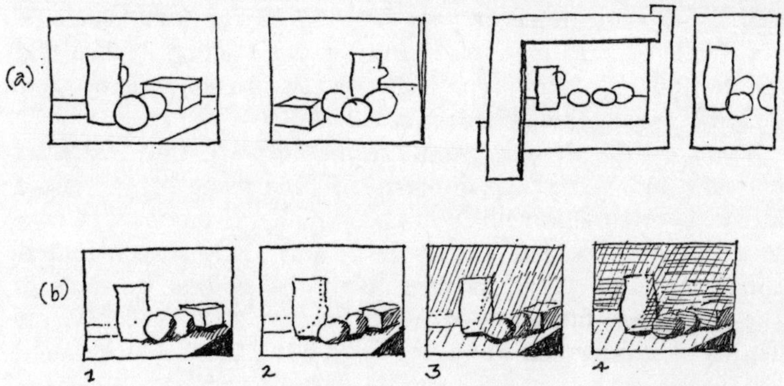

FIG. 3 (a) *Arranging the objects of the still life in a rectangle.* (b) *1. Darkest shapes. 2. Lightest shapes. 3. Light middle-tone shapes. 4. Dark middle-tone shapes.*

angles on the still life. Another important aspect of relationships is not only the objects with each other, but also everything within the confines of the four edges of the painting. You cannot really consider objects just floating somehow. Spaces round objects are also very important. Next time, when you draw for a

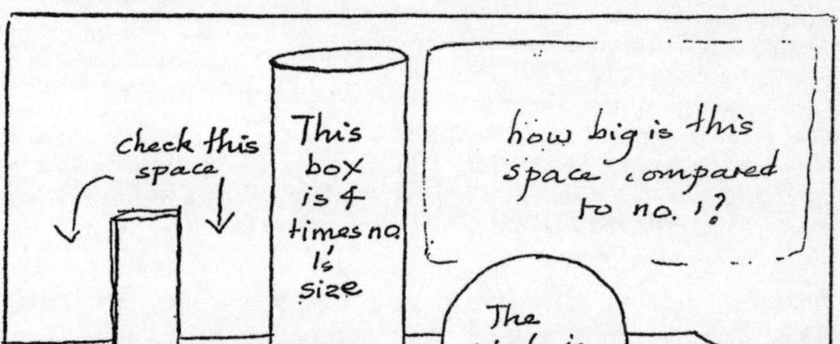

FIG. 4 *Supposing you took this object as the norm of proportion and measured every other by it.*

still life, confine some of your drawings in the same shape (if not the same size) that you intend for the painting. Notice that the amount of space round the objects in an enclosed area makes a considerable difference to them.

Light and shade. All colours lie between the tonal extremes of black and white, a point that has been made before, and a fact you are familiar with from photography. If the tonal balance of a picture is wrong it distorts the colour. There are some interchangeable aspects of tonality. With the objects in front of you, transpose them into what you believe their colour values are between black and white (see Figs. 5 and 3 (b)). For instance,

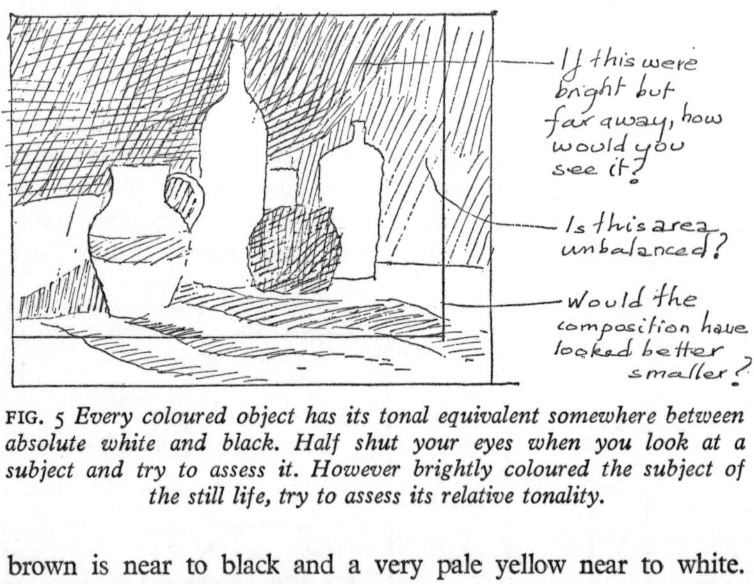

FIG. 5 *Every coloured object has its tonal equivalent somewhere between absolute white and black. Half shut your eyes when you look at a subject and try to assess it. However brightly coloured the subject of the still life, try to assess its relative tonality.*

brown is near to black and a very pale yellow near to white. This is a very good way of training your eye to see tone. You will find some strange paradoxes. For tone can be used to create extension in depth. The nearer an object is to you the stronger the colour. But a paradox lies when you find there is a bright background in the distance and a dull object close to. In an another exercise you see that tonality can create roundness and this affects colour. What may appear in line as a balanced drawing may be distorted by tones. If you can think in tone it is easy to think in colour.

Drawing the still life is something you can, and should do the whole time in a little sketch book, and you will be surprised at the number of times the things around you suddenly become delightful compositions. Do not forget that all painting is composition. Draw some oddments, put a rectangle round them, and here they are, enclosed in the little world you have made for them. If this sounds banal I am glad, it was meant to. But if *you do it* the banal will become special and this is what painting is about.

Drawing for painting. Before starting a painting you will probably want to explore it by drawing. Thus, most of this chapter and the one on basic design, are very much concerned with designing the picture as a whole. In general once the design of a picture holds together it can carry weaknesses of detail. But for all this, to you as a beginner, some objects that take your fancy for the still life may be difficult to draw, or objects not so difficult to draw may be in odd positions. So let us look at some things for which you may have to make separate studies (Fig. 6). You can see it is a question of finding the general shape and breaking it down to its parts. The other problem is how forms become distorted, particularly in the case of plants and flowers. See Fig. 56.

Study whatever drawings, old and new, that appeal to you. Remember there are an infinite number of ways of doing good drawings and only about three ways of doing bad ones. When you study drawings of experienced artists you might think I have reduced drawing to rules that are not worth bothering about. But it is only when you have learned the idea of a system of rules that you can create your own system.

Now for controversy. Even if you never paint anything but a still life look at the greatest drawings of all, figures by Michelangelo and Raphael. None of us will equal them, but we can always learn from them.

Extension continued. The other ways of creating extension are acting upon the cultural conventions that we in the western world acquire as children from illustrations and posters. It would appear that since Roman times a formula for extension into space has been light and shadow, and this was transmitted by force of convention till its dramatic recreation by Giotto. This convention is the illusion of solid form by means of light and shadow (Fig. 7). It means accepting the conventions, one of them

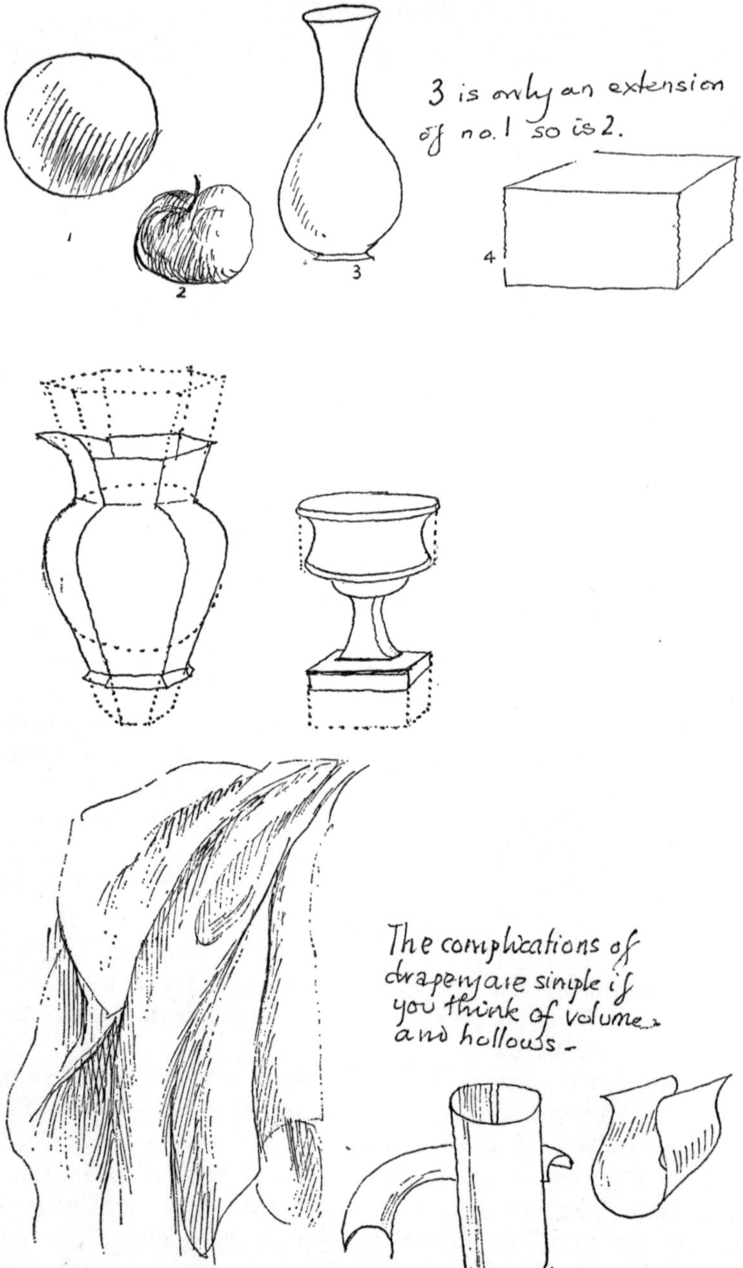

FIG. 6 *Complicated objects are easy to draw if you simplify them first.*

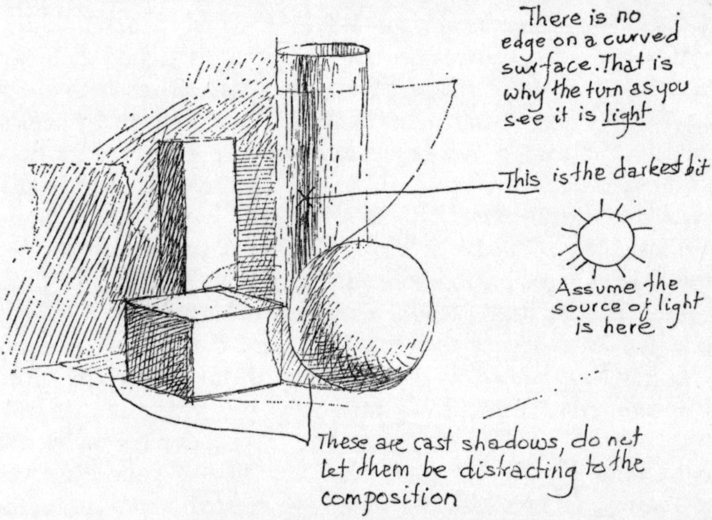

FIG. 7 *Light and shade as the language of solid form. More than one source of light makes for difficulties.*

being that the source of light is consistent. This does not exclude shadow as compositional pattern, as the paintings of the high Baroque show us. It is true to say that you can paint just as well without this system. It is worthwhile, at first, to distinguish between what might be called the incidents of cast shadow as against the shadows that create form. A beginner to still life has to be particularly careful not to get carried away by the incidents of cast shadow. This convention is useful in the figure, the still life, the interior and portrait, while you may need it in landscape, but possibly less so. The creation of shadow to effect solid form should not be thought of as something that you can dress up a weak drawing with to hide its incompetence. You will not get away with this for long. It is to be used primarily because some artists instinctively model form solidly, then for emphasis, and equally important for tonal pattern.

Perspective. Another convention that we have in the west is that of perspective. This too, may have been known in classical times, but the perspective we know today is traditionally attributed to Brunelleschi, the founder of Renaissance architecture. From that it developed into a highly complex science, and there are countless examples in the Renaissance when an architect-artist (rightly, then there was not so rigid a distinction as today) has painted a perspective extension of a hall. Bramante, in the Church of Presso San Satiro in Milan, has done so by logical extension, and so convincingly that you are never aware of it at first. Leonardo in his *Last Supper*, Milan, has slightly distorted the logical extension. So what then is the logical basis? The basis of perspective is taking the axiomatic assumption that parallel lines meet on the horizon. Perspective need not be complicated, and in itself is not. Think of looking down a railroad track, the lines appear to meet. Of course they cannot possibly meet, but supposing you tried to draw them not meeting. You go up hill. Maybe you are going to say you prefer it that way, if you do no need to read on, but if you don't look at the diagrams in Fig. 8. Assume a horizon, that is your eye-level, and the rest follows logically. You have created a convention for the linear representation of space. You have to accept the first axiom (unlcss you are one of those people who thinks it's clever to argue about anything and everything). The same rules apply if you draw looking straight, head on, into a room. A complication arises when looking into a corner of a room because you

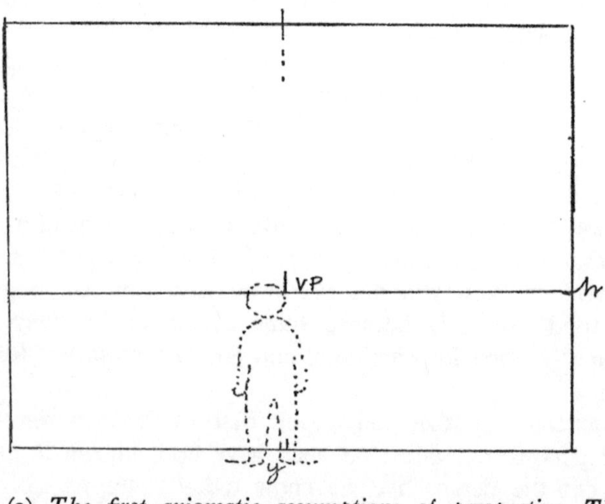

FIG. 8 (a) *The first axiomatic assumptions of perspective. The line of your eyes is the horizon=h, you are at* y, *where you are looking is the vanishing point=*VP.

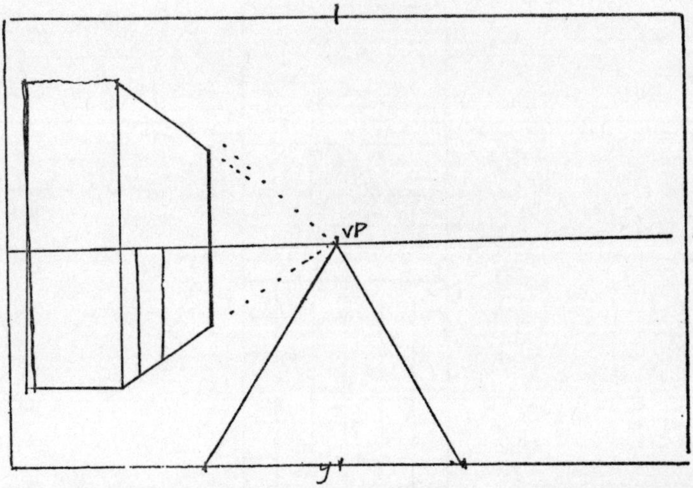

FIG. 8 (b) *So if you are looking down a rail track, the parallel lines appear to meet at* VP. *In effect, lines* above *your eye slope down to the horizon, lines below the horizon slope* up *to meet it. All else now follows.*

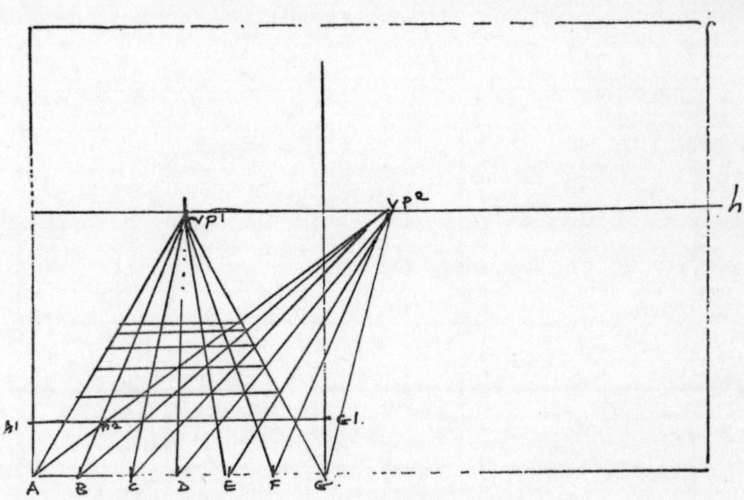

FIG. 8 (c) *A tiled floor in perspective showing head-on and angled view. To draw the angled view let distance* A *to* A¹=*distance* A *to* B. *Let* G *to* G¹=*distance* A *to* B. *Join* A¹ *to* G¹. *Join* A *to* A² *and extend to* VP² *on horizon. Join* B,C,D,E,F *and* G *to* VP².

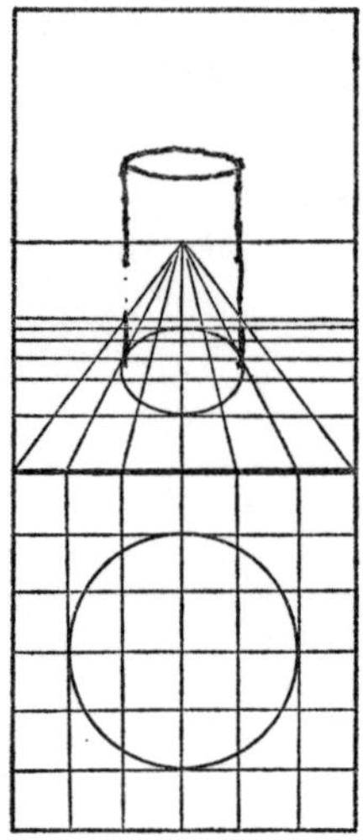

FIG. 8 (d) *A circle in perspective.*

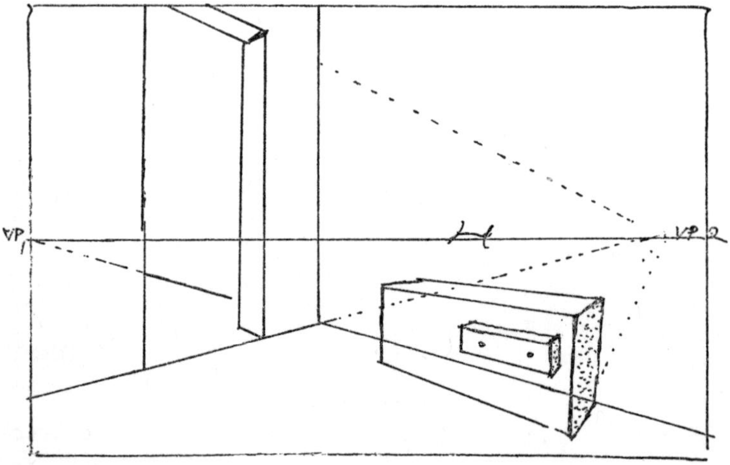

FIG. 8 (e) *Looking into a corner of a room you get two vanishing points.*

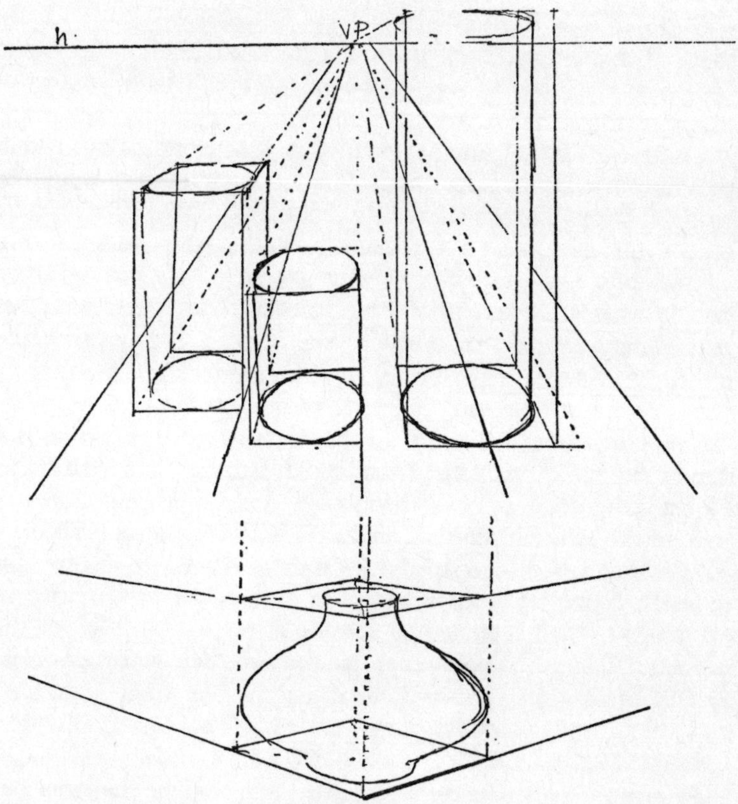

FIG. 8 (f) *To draw a cylindrical form in perspective, draw a cube first.*

get two vanishing points, but again the same basic rules apply (see Fig. 8(e)). Figs. 8(d) and (f) show how to deal with circles and cylinders, but a sphere always remains unchanged.

Once assuming the basic rule of perspective you can play rather amusing games by inverting, as it were, the logic, and you may be familiar with the engravings of Escher, an artist who takes the conventions of creating a logical space, caricatures and inverts them to an amazing degree. This is playing jolly games, and have fun, but really we have set about learning to paint. Exaggerated perspective is an extraordinarily useful device in technical drawing but scarcely the concern here. It is as well to get the handling of the basic grammar of perspective if you can so that it is automatic. I say 'if you can' because I can think of many very good painters who either cannot understand perspective, or feel that it does not enter into their scheme of things. Perhaps the words of Constable apply here, they apply most times: 'Every original picture is a separate study, and is governed by laws of its own. What is right in one would be entirely wrong if transferred to another.' Within the picture space you have to be consistent, creating the picture's own autonomous universe. This is why, on page 162 I've said you can do what you like with colour, painting skies green and grass red, it may be right in terms of the picture. We have strayed rather from perspective. Verbal description does not get us very far, it is a visual science. Looking at quattrocento paintings we can be fairly sure that many a complicated special extension was drawn by many an artist who could neither read nor write. Perhaps the greatest of all handbooks for the artist is Alberti's treatise on painting, finished in 1436. This is now published by Yale University in a paperback, and you can get a copy for yourself. A far cry from Alberti's original which was written in manuscript, itself intended as a work of art as much as for the contents. 'He who looks at a picture will see a certain cross section of a visual pyramid, artificially represented with lines and colours on a certain plane according to a given distance, centre and lights.'

Drawing details. Cones, blocks, etc., you may be thinking, but the ingredients of the still life are far more complex than this if you think of all the kinds of jugs, and fruits, etc. The fact is that details are never the problem. One often sees in the life class a student drawing a complex detail of a face. The reason, as the tutor is always told, is that this detail is experiment or analysis. Maybe, but the fact is that it is usually a justification for not getting to grips with the whole, always the problem is synthesis and breadth. So once you can make a fair drawing of cubes and cones the more complex steps will come easily, as they are variants on these anyway (see Fig. 6).

The traditional art-school training used to be from geometric shapes to the antique, and then to the life class. It became in many art schools an end in itself and appeared to cramp the vision of many a gifted student. This system was abolished in most art schools in the western world, with a horrifying destruction of valuable plaster casts. What happened was that it made very little difference to whether a student became an artist or not, and in many cases gifted artists suffered. One has never heard of any writer in English whose primal vision was destroyed by learning Latin.

The Antique. We all are familiar with the word 'Renaissance'. As likely as not in its rather debased interpretation vaguely meaning a revival of ideas and culture. The correct usage means the revival of the learning of Greece and Rome, most associated with the city states of Italy in the fifteenth, sixteenth and seventeenth centuries. Looking at works of art of these times it is not at all difficult to see where an artist has quoted an antique image, sometimes as a mythology or transposed into a Christian context. The *Venus Pudica,* with a change of the gesture of the head becomes, in Masaccio's fresco, Eve after the fall. Many minor masters of the sixteenth century put the Cumaean Sibyl in nativity groups associating Christ's birth with Virgil's *IVth Eclogue.* We read Petrarch's marvellously moving account of copying Cicero by hand, to have his own copy before the invention of the printing press. Centuries after Virgil's lifetime, in his birthplace Mantua, the fifteenth-century painter Mantegna paints a Triumph of Caesar. Virgil and Mantegna are greater than Caesar. In the Renaissance many antique statues were known of from Pliny's descriptions in his *Natural History.* When these, or copies, were found they were greeted with unprecedented jubilation. But none of this has described why there was this intensification of classical studies at this time. It might be inaccurate to suggest total rebirth as many scholars rightly see unbroken tradition from classical antiquity through the Middle Ages. Why then? This could almost be unanswerable. So much phenomena that time condenses into a historical period, can have no one explanation, but many. This is where we as artists come in, for, we as artists can find the most immediate reason for the revival of antiquity – that the antiques are proportionate, noble and lovely. Drawing the antiques has the same appeal as learning a classical language. The appeal is not immediate (though you may be one of those happy and special people for whom it is) to everyone. You like it through doing it, you do not gratify an appetite. Only by drawing the antique can you realise why it was once the foundation of all artists' studies. Most of us are obliged to draw from plaster-cast originals which have a rather dead surface, but they retain at least the proportions and lines of the originals. Like some still life objects, the antiques have the same characteristics, they do not move and you can keep on and on at the same subject till you get it right.

We could approach the antique historically, starting with archaic statues, getting more and more lifelike, which is the progress of Greek sculpture. It would seem that a primal simple model was compared to real life. In the last seventy years the archaic Greek statues have enjoyed far more popularity than the more lifelike and graceful sculptures of the age of Phideas and Praxiteles, as the archaic had more in common with primitive culture which has so affected twentieth-century art and psychology. This can all too easily lead to the idea that if a drawing is crude, or frankly inept, it has a primitive vigour. But of course you cannot decide to be a primitive, this very type of conscious choice means that you are not. From the Greeks we could go on to the Romans. With the Romans we get a bit of a complication for many of the things that were believed to be Greek in Renaissance times are now known to be Roman copies of Greek originals, and moreover, bad copies at that. We cannot know, but this reflects on another contemporary fad to believe quite unfairly, that Roman sculpture is a debasement of Greek, simply it is not. Greek sculpture is of gods, mostly, and Roman of men, and speaks to us now in as different a language as Homer from Cicero.

If ever you have moments of doubt, as all artists do, or wonder if it's true what people say about painting not being immediately useful, there can be nothing more valuable in an uncertain time than individuals preserving and handing down some aspect of that very ore of our cultural traditions, the classics. Art and its history are inseparable.

Where to find antiques. You may be lucky enough to live near a major museum which may have its own collection, or a collection of casts. Otherwise a local art school may still have some.

Having found your first statue, take pencil, board and paper. Not too big a drawing, about double the size of your fist. Fig. 9 shows an archaic Kouros, as this type of statue was called. It probably dates from the sixth century and was intended for a

FIG. 9 *An archaic Kouros. You can start drawing from a geometric schema.*

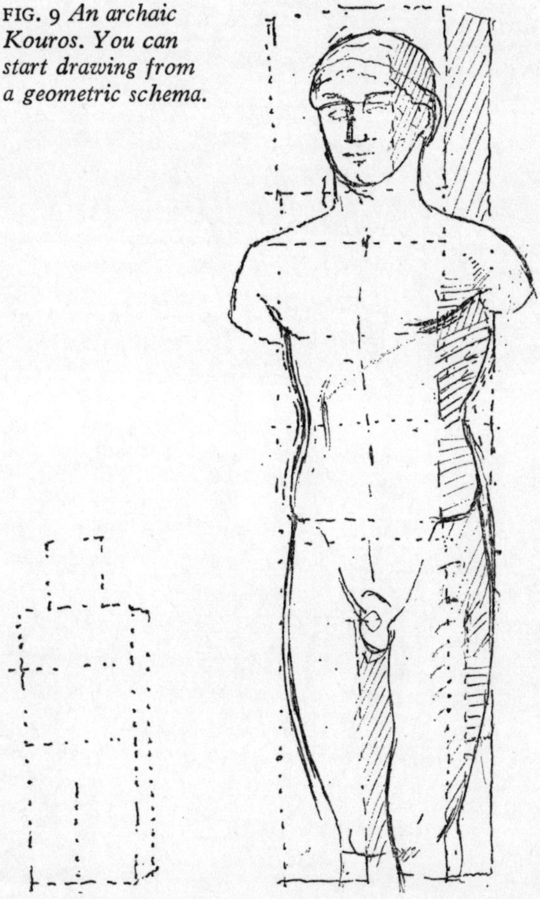

sanctuary or grave. Walking round it as you should you can see that it has very definite front, two sides and a back. We could start then with our schema of a double cube, or build up the whole from small geometric units. You should draw from the three angles, building up from geometric shapes makes a reasonable beginning. But remember that it is rather easy to get into the manner of building up drawings of the animate from blocks and while one has seen paintings of life done this way, it isn't very attractive.

The next statue (Fig. 10) is an advance. Instead of the pose stepping straight forwardly it has developed towards the most

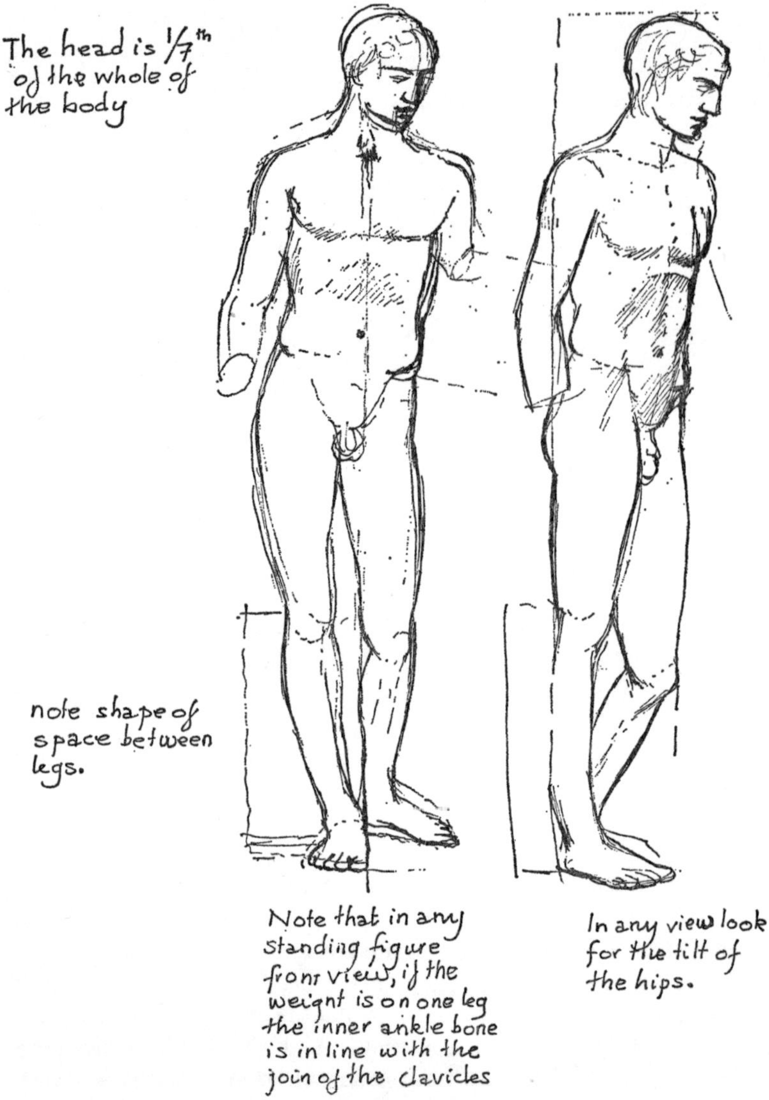

FIG. 10 *An advanced Kouros.*

typical of classical statues, the weight resting on one leg. This gives a most subtle swing to the body, to the extent that the planes of the body are now no longer sharply defined into sides, front and back. You could begin your drawing with the double cube, if it was useful. Or else, as many a Greek artist did, see how many times the head went into the body. Another usual proportion was the length of the foot, how many times is this multiplied in the length of the body. But, how to get the swing of the body? You could begin by drawing the hips. Or by carefully drawing the exact space between the feet and working up the drawing from that. It is not easy for you, me or anyone. The next thing you could try is another traditional device, a plumb (from lead) line. Tie a weight of some description to a piece of string about as long as your forearm (it must be a heavy weight). The line you hold up will fall vertically. All lines off the vertical will be conspicuous. In fact, you are taking the vertical as a sort of norm. Now, hold the plumb line up in front of the statue at the inner ankle bone of the leg carrying the weight. You will find that the pit of the neck is directly in line with it, and this is a constant of classical statues. Mark in this line gently, and you can measure all other variants from the vertical and horizontal from this.

Measurement. A fashion more from English art schools than any other has been this way of building up drawings entirely by measurement. It can give the drawing the appearance of clinical detachment, and can very easily become an unattractive mannerism. Of course measurements are useful, but not as an end in themselves.

The Apollo Belvedere (Fig. 11). Once the most celebrated of all the antiques. It has inspired directly countless works of art, among them Raphael's figure of Christ in the cartoon *Feed my Sheep,* then Titian's Bacchus in *Bacchus and Ariadne*. Michelangelo transforms it to be Adam in the Sistine ceiling. Yet, to copy directly, it eludes us. Try drawing it. If the merest line is out then all is out. The hint of a proportion that is wrong and it appears clumsy and ridiculous. Off the correct balance, and it falls over. How to draw? I believe, but do it your way, that finally one must return to outline. Of course, outline doesn't mean just a confining enclosure, line can be varied to give emphasis and recession. But keep trying, when you have got somewhere near you will probably be able to draw anything. So beautifully proportionate are the classical male gods, that if any line is out it is not the merest thing, it is the all. You can

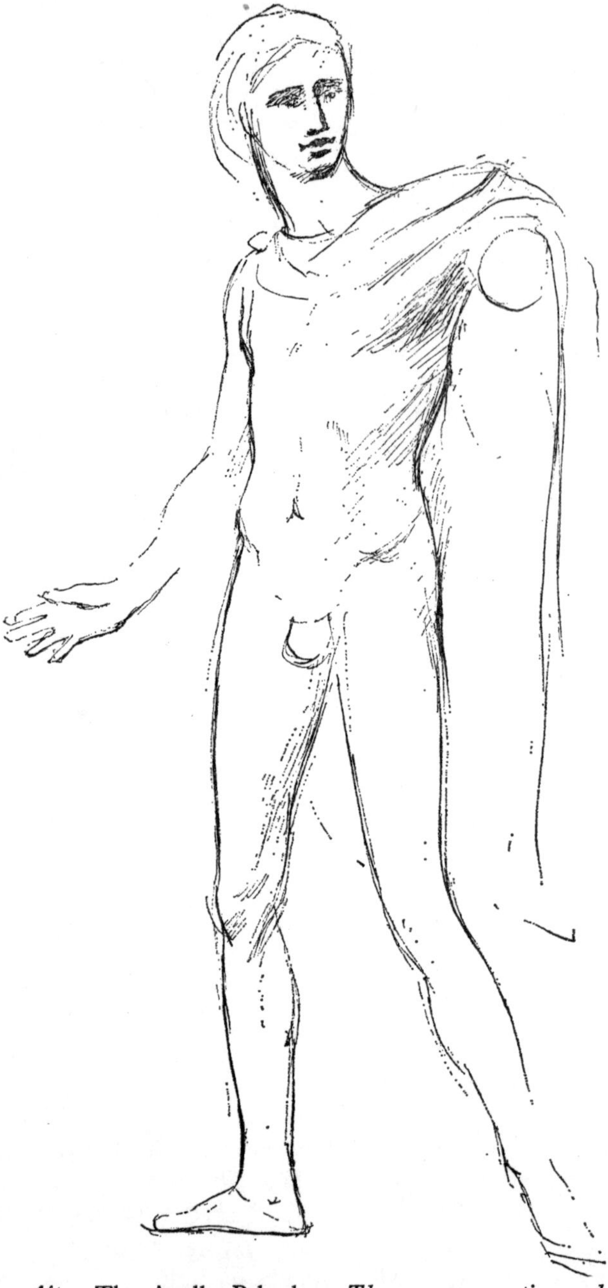

FIG. 11 *After* The Apollo Belvedere. *There comes a time when the artist must abandon measurements and instruments, and rely only on his eye and line.*

see that this gives an inflexible approach to drawing from life itself. To tell yourself in front of an antique that your drawing is out of proportion because of deliberate intent or some experiment, just doesn't ring true. *The Apollo Belvedere* is a Roman copy of a Greek bronze original, while it must have looked truly amazing in the original material, the copy we have was made with a true artist's eye and hand. Belvedere is a reference to the residence in the Vatican of its first owner and patron of the arts, Pope Julius II.

From gods to men and some rather less exacting things to draw. The Romans have left us some fine portrait heads (see Fig. 12). You have drawn apples, you have drawn spheres and cubes. So here you go. When you start think of the simple clear shapes. A bit of alteration, measuring and variation and, here you are, you have a head. Not quite a likeness? A bit of measurement will soon put that right. It has a silly expression? A bit more difficult, for the merest line out and that's what you get. But take heart, you do not have a model who moves or gets tired. Check the position of the eyes and mouth in relation to the whole of the head. Now concentrate on the vital inner line between the lips. There you are, you have a likeness. When next you have to draw a head or an apple neither will be too formidable.

The above, it is true, does not include the countless seated figures and animals that are part of our heritage of antique statuary. It is no reflection of course on their beauty and merit. It is more a question that once you can make a reasonable drawing of a figure with the weight of the body on one leg, all else is comparatively easy. The last things that are instructive and pleasing to study tie up with modelling. We have seen that one of the traditions of western art, inextricably bound with the classical tradition, is modelling with light and dark. Known to the ancients, rediscovered through direct craftsman's tradition by Giotto, it is more than likely that this convention was discovered by looking at light falling on reliefs.

Relief statuary was a major art of all the ancient and classical peoples. The gravestones and tombs of the Romans gave a vocabulary of visual rhetorical form to the European tradition. Then there are the reliefs on monuments, like the Parthenon frieze, that give us a whole picture of a people. To end, let us

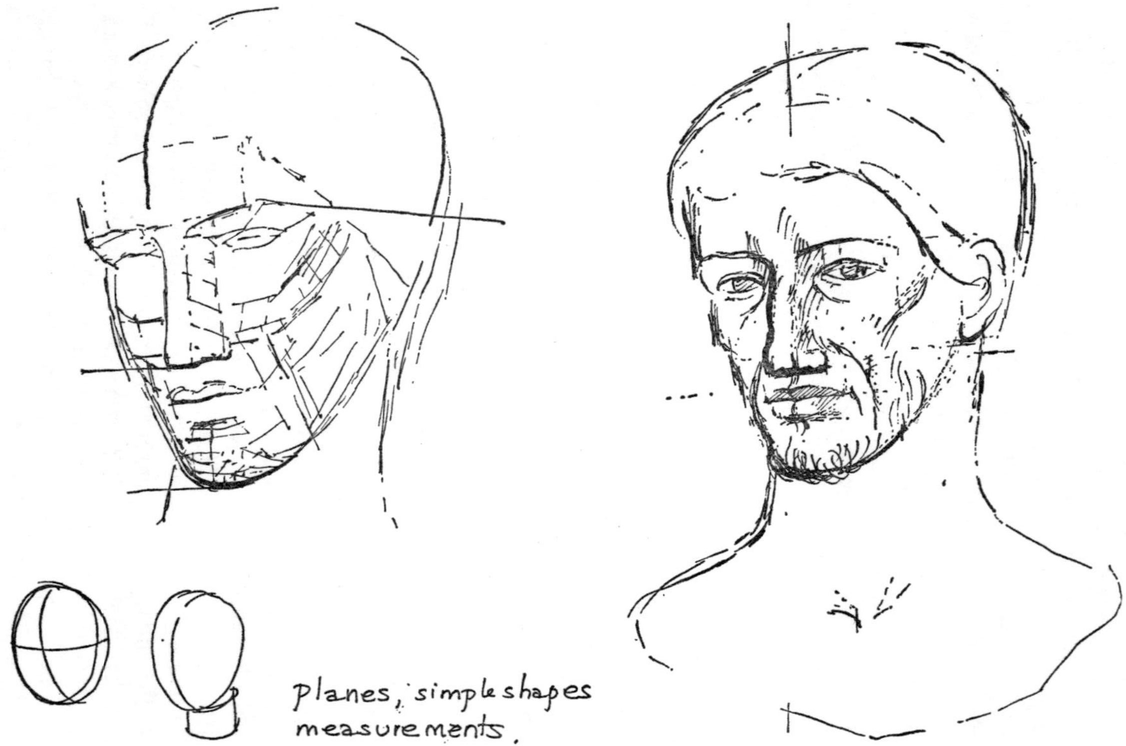

FIG. 12 *Roman bust.*

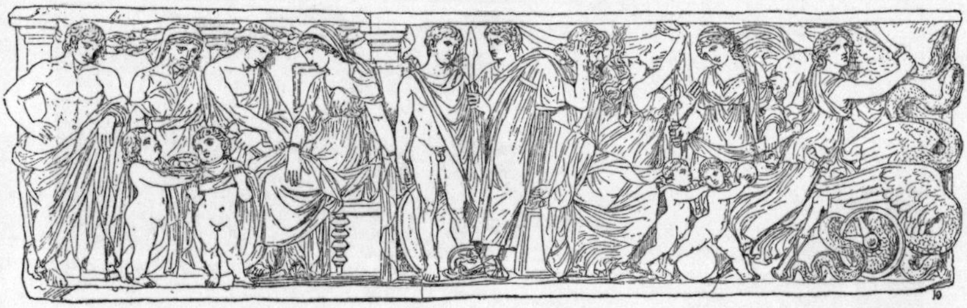

(a)

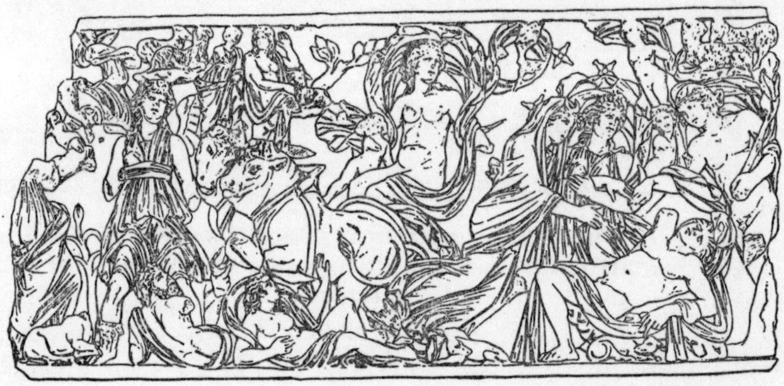

(b)

FIG. 13 (a) *Sarcophagus of Medea, Greece.* (b) *Sarcophagus of Endymion, Rome.*

compare and draw two, one from Greece and the other from Rome (see Fig. 13).

The earliest accounts of Masaccio and Giotto, who painted such marvellously solid figures, describe them as though they imitated the real. Like the anecdote in which Giotto paints a fly so realistically that somebody attempted to brush it off. In effect then solid modelling extends outward to us. The other use of tone as extension is the other way about. To make tone effect distance. We have seen perspective creating distance. To use tone to make distance, with or without linear perspective, is not difficult. It takes the basic assumption that the nearer an object is to you the greater the intensity of the dark tones, the further away the paler the tones and the less the contrast be-

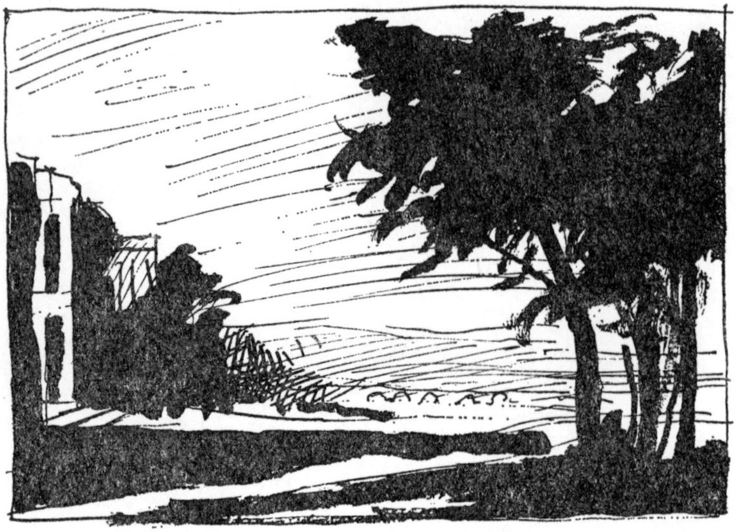

FIG. 14 *In this, after a print from Claude Lorraine, the dark and light contrasts are for nearness. The distance loses intensity of colour and tone.*

tween absolute darks and lights (Fig. 14). This is more applicable in landscape than in still life.

A footnote for those of you who really find composition difficult. There is an easy way out and if you are only painting for fun and want to make life easy all the way round, here it is. Take two L-shaped pieces of cardboard, move them about, vary the shape over your drawing or hold them up to your eye, and there you are, you have your composition (Fig. 15). With

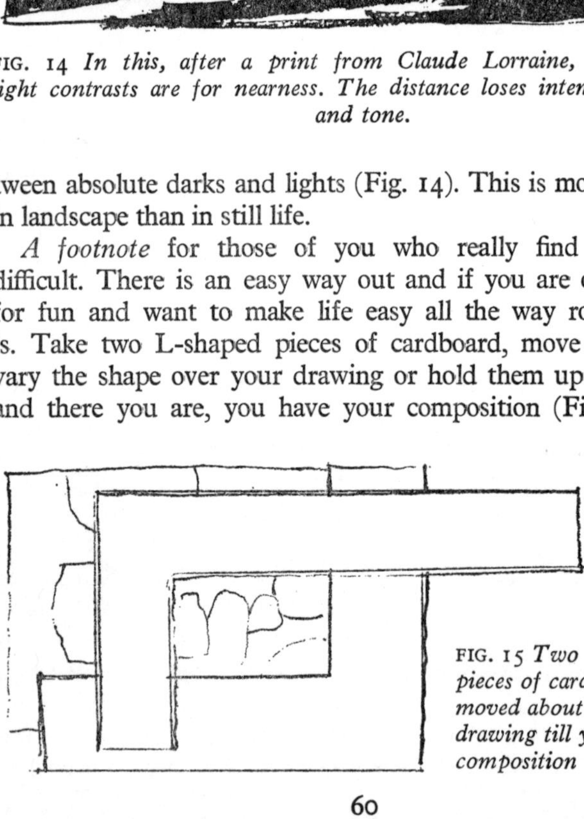

FIG. 15 *Two L-shaped pieces of cardboard can be moved about over a drawing till you find a composition you like.*

practice though, in the end, you will almost see ready-made pictures around you.

A final practicality. Squaring up. This is a means of transferring a drawing to a board, canvas, wall, or anything else. The principle is of congruent triangles. It can be done by squares which is more trouble and no more nor less effective, unless, like Sickert used to, you have drawn on squared paper anyway. Please yourself about the need to square up. It is not really necessary unless you are transferring a really small drawing to a large area. Fig. 16 explains the method.

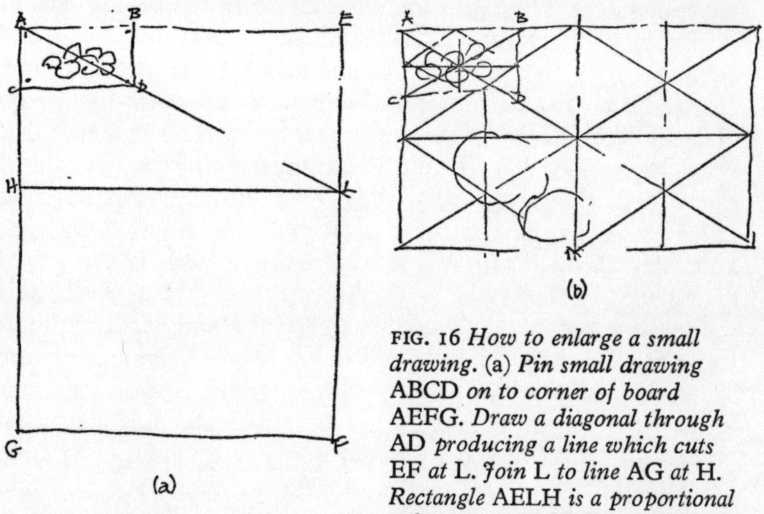

FIG. 16 *How to enlarge a small drawing.* (a) *Pin small drawing* ABCD *on to corner of board* AEFG. *Draw a diagonal through* AD *producing a line which cuts* EF *at* L. *Join* L *to line* AG *at* H. *Rectangle* AELH *is a proportional enlargement of* ABCD. (b) *By proportional increase of grid on larger area you can transfer a smaller drawing exactly.*

CHAPTER 4

Basic Design and the Still Life

A painting without drawing is like an opera without any tunes. No amount of dressing up and colour will disguise the lack of it, for long. There are levels of melody, some very great and subtle, others good and obvious; and it is like that with drawing. If you have read the introduction there is a remark that many of us arrange things on shelves, or set out a table in a way that is pleasing and this is not irrelevant to drawing. Much of drawing is about this very thing, the pleasing disposition of shapes, in terms of contrast, balance and various rhythms. For a painter this all adds up to composition. This is the art of giving unity of concept to the picture space, that within this space there can be any amount of diversity and yet it all holds together. We shall see there are many ways of giving a picture unity. The idea behind most of the experiments in this chapter is the unity of the picture space. To a beginner this may seem an insurmountable difficulty but it is only a question of forming habits of seeing. After regular practice in design you will find that whatever you are looking at you will see a composition. As many beginners are not full-time artists most exercises are planned so that they can be done in spare moments. The contemporary term for this aspect of drawing is basic design, hence the title of the chapter. Arranging shapes can be easily learned so even if you feel you have no natural aptitude let us start now.

You will need ordinary white cartridge paper and a pencil, or pen and ink. On the paper draw several rectangles. In the chapter on drawing we studied the *calligraphic* aspect of line (see Fig. 2). Now for another aspect.

Line as division.

1. Divide the first rectangle by a vigorous line vertically down the centre (see Fig. 17). The spaces are now equally balanced.

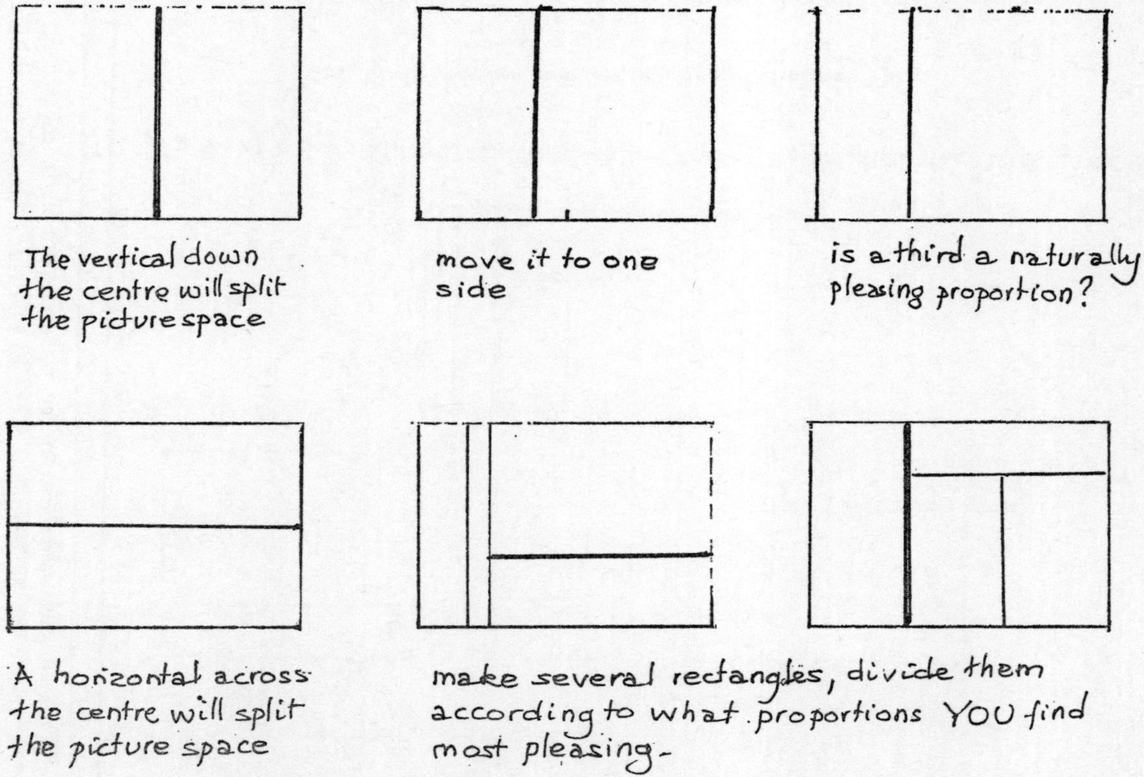

FIG. 17 (a) *Using line to divide the picture space.*

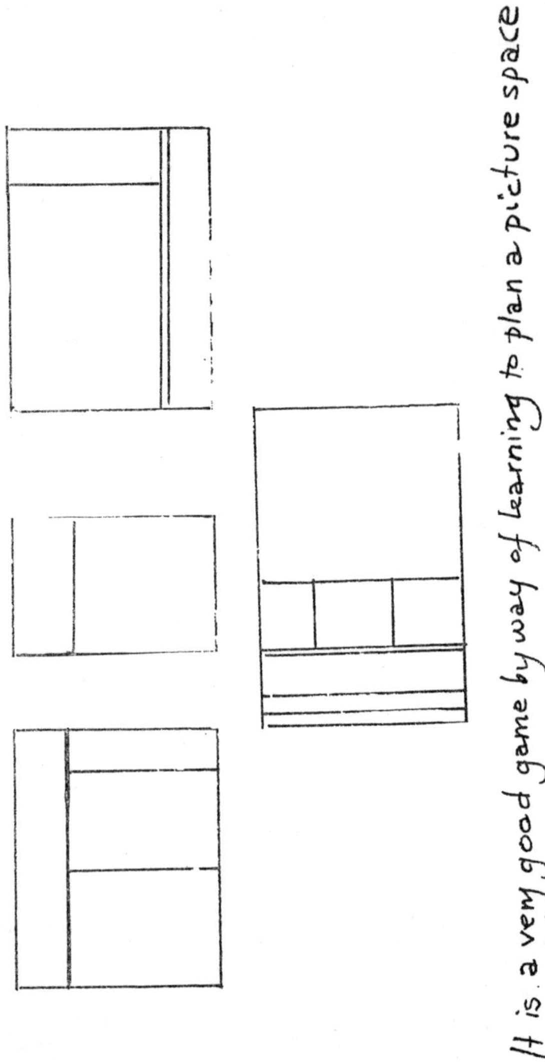

FIG. 17 (b) *Further exercises in planning a picture space.*

Would it give more life to the picture space if, in the second rectangle, the dividing line were to one side? Or, at the third of the space instead of the half?

2. Now, divide the spaces in the rectangles with horizontal lines. You will find that any line that cuts the rectangle completely in half makes two separate spaces. Are you now reminded of

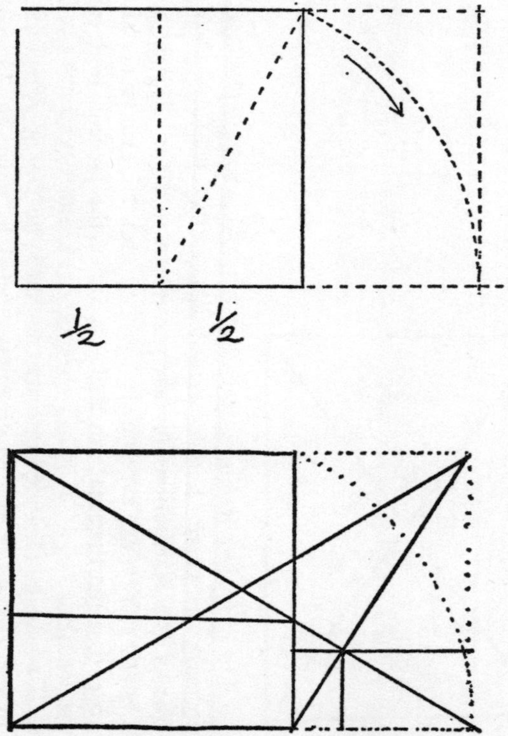

FIG. 18 *The Golden Section.*

Mondrian's vigorous and lively compositions? You often hear people say that anyone could have done them, but these few sketches should have demonstrated otherwise.

3. If you are finding it a pleasing and amusing game dividing up rectangles like this, why not try a full-scale painting?

4. You could try the classic exercise of the so-called 'Golden Section' (Fig. 18). This is a proportion especially typical of those painter-architects like Piero, Alberti and Bramante.

Looking at the diagram you can see that it is easy to do with just a peg and string. You can make satisfying shapes and divisions without any other skill.

You will see that designing a space is as much about what is left out! As well as being reminded of Mondrian you could be thinking of modern buildings. This is one of the great lessons of modern basic design. It teaches us to look for the fundamental principles of design which apply to every object made by the hand of man. In the chapter on flowers the aspect of basic pattern in the context of nature will be discussed. To go on to the next line divisions and these are diagonals.

1. If you join the diagonal from two corners, again the picture is split, and it is this that will dominate the picture space, whatever else you try to do. See Fig. 19.

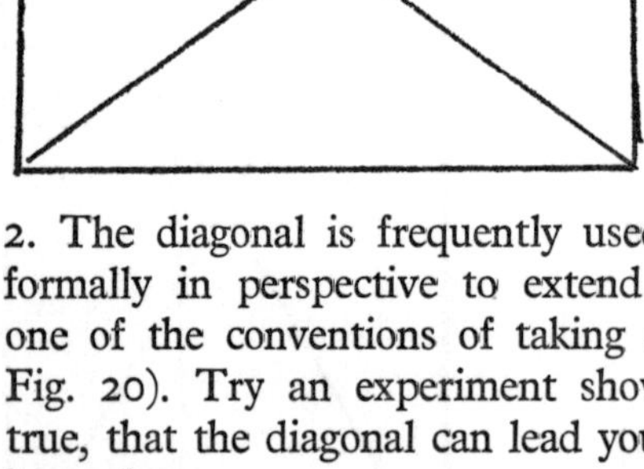

FIG. 19 *Diagonals can split and centre a space.*

2. The diagonal is frequently used in compositions. It is used formally in perspective to extend space. The diagonal is also one of the conventions of taking our eye into the picture (see Fig. 20). Try an experiment showing that the reverse is also true, that the diagonal can lead you out of the picture. Both can be useful.

Two diagonals meeting, and you have the feeling of stability in the triangular composition, very usual in portraits. In land-

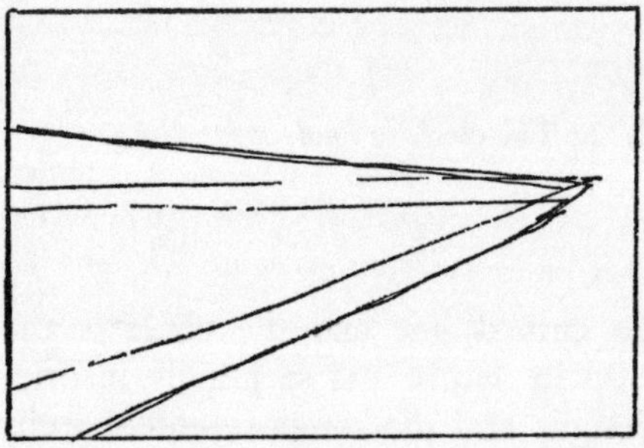

FIG. 20 *Diagonals can lead you into a picture space. Take care they don't lead you out too.*

scape, figure composition and still life, the triangle can lead and fix your eye on a specific point (Fig. 21). If straight lines and horizontal lines are static then the diagonal variations can give us an agitated rhythm. Once a motif is repeated you get rhythm and pattern. This is dealt with at more length below.

The circle as basic design. A circle having no beginning nor end is complete in itself, having no angles the eye has no resting place (Fig. 22). It is different in character and flavour from the curved line which gives movement. A curved line is rhythmic in itself and gives the feeling of movement less agitated than the

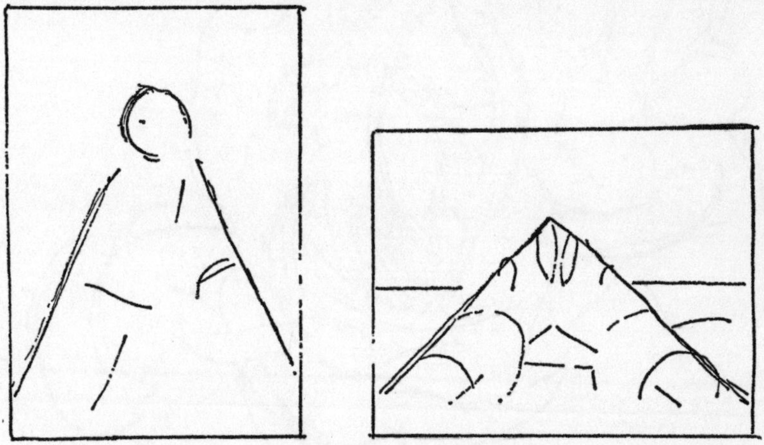

FIG. 21 (a) *Upright triangular composition to effect stability. Many an Old Master used it in portraits and altarpieces.* (b) *The longwise triangle for monumentality. Think of Raphael's Vatican frescoes, and Cézanne's mountain landscapes.*

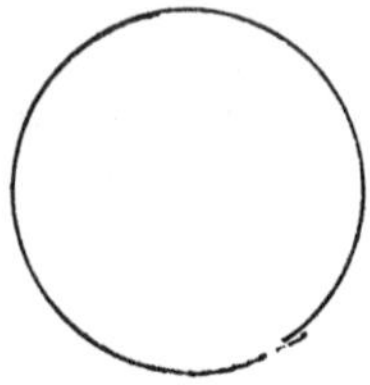

FIG. 22 *The circle is final, compelling.*

diagonal. A variation of the curved line and the circle is the spiral, a pattern that turns up in nature and seemingly instinctively in many traditional designs and the compositions of well-known paintings (Fig. 23).

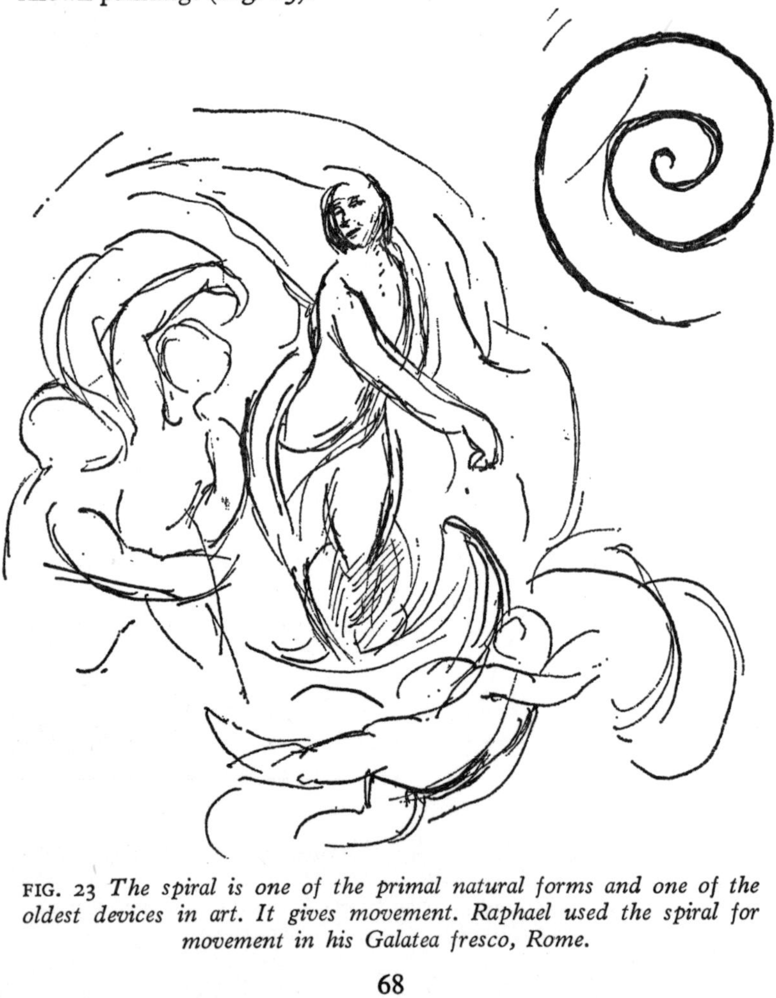

FIG. 23 *The spiral is one of the primal natural forms and one of the oldest devices in art. It gives movement. Raphael used the spiral for movement in his Galatea fresco, Rome.*

It is in these rhythms that we can draw the most valid analogies between music and painting. Rhythms are based on repetition and it is the character of the repetition that, like music, can evoke a mood – a slow and solemn rhythm, or an ecstatic one. It can be rhythmic with accents as well, like the beat in the bar.

Repetition is worth exploring. It is a very important aspect of design in the applied arts, like textiles, pottery and architecture. Fig. 24 gives some examples of how to design by repetition, which means dividing the rectangles of the picture space in the above ways by drawn lines. This is one way of designing, the other way is by . . .

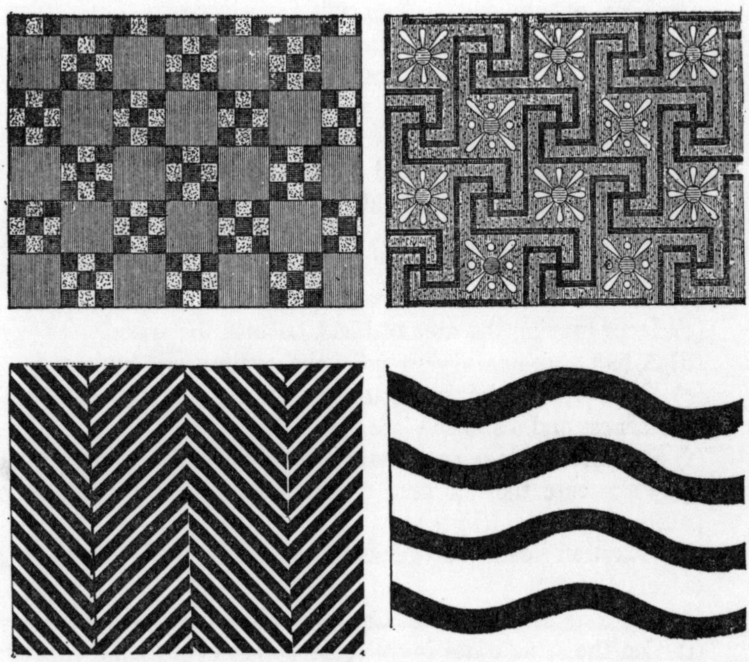

(a)

(b)

FIG. 24 (a) *Design by repetition.* (b) *Rhythm by repetition.*

Tone and shape. Tone is a very important aspect of design and painting. Practically, the tone of a colour is how it relates to the extremes of black and white. Like if you take a photograph of a patterned textile you get the black and white equivalents. The same applies to paintings; if a highly coloured painting is reproduced in black and white the tonal values can, in a good painting, give the photograph much of the life and vitality of the original; tone then is inseparable from colour. If in the course of reading this you find that terms of classification are interchangeable, this is as it should be, for the classifications are not for rigid definition, but only to conveniently isolate specific points. *Shape* in this context is rather like the children's toy you have all had or seen where simple areas of colour are called shapes. Put on a background they make their own outline as contrasted with a drawn outline. Now for designing with tone and shape.

For this you will need black and white poster paint, water, a mixing palette and an inexpensive paintbrush. On a piece of cartridge paper draw a series of empty rectangles. The illustrations in Fig. 25 will give you some ideas. These may seem like exercises, but an artist can no more overlook exercises than a musician can. How many of us look at a musician performing, the centre of admiration and attention, and wish to be like that? We should also want to be like the musician when he is practising hour after hour.

(a) Does a small area of black dominate the space?
(b) Does an area of white balance it?
(c) Does moving the area of black balance the space?
(d) A half-way line always splits the picture (see Fig. 17).
(e) Does dark in the foreground receding to light give the feeling of nearness and distance? (see Fig. 14).
(f) Evenness of tone can destroy the vitality of a painting.
(g) Take care that no area or shape dominates the centre of a painting.
(h) Rhythm can be achieved through tonal balance and dispersal.
(i) Use tone as expression. Can even tones express calm?
(j) Can the same tones in different shapes express the opposite?

If you liked you could turn some of these sketches into full-scale paintings. You will then find that size of areas of tone or colour affects their impact. You may be thinking that this has not much to do with still life which is the title of the book. Basic design should underlie any aspect of painting. Indeed, in a historical context abstraction is allied to still life. Think of the purely abstract paintings of Ben Nicholson and Braque. These were a natural evolution from the still lifes of the cubist painters. The cubists' approach to still life was not sitting in front of the natural object and painting it. Instead, well-known objects in our everyday experience were the starting point of painting. The artists varied these objects many ways without them losing their identity. It was through the extreme simplification in these paintings that pure abstract paintings evolved. Some of the motifs designed by the cubist painters gave enormous inspiration to designers of posters, books and textiles. Working in a reverse way, we have looked at basic abstract design. In the previous chapter you have drawn from nature, so with these you could start designing from the man-made object. When you think of

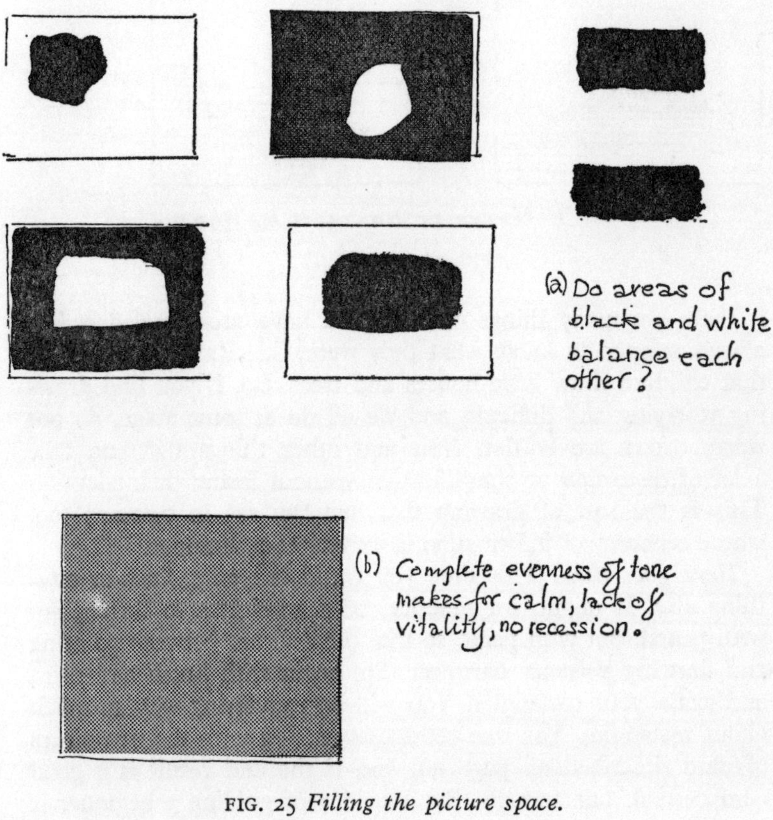

FIG. 25 *Filling the picture space.*

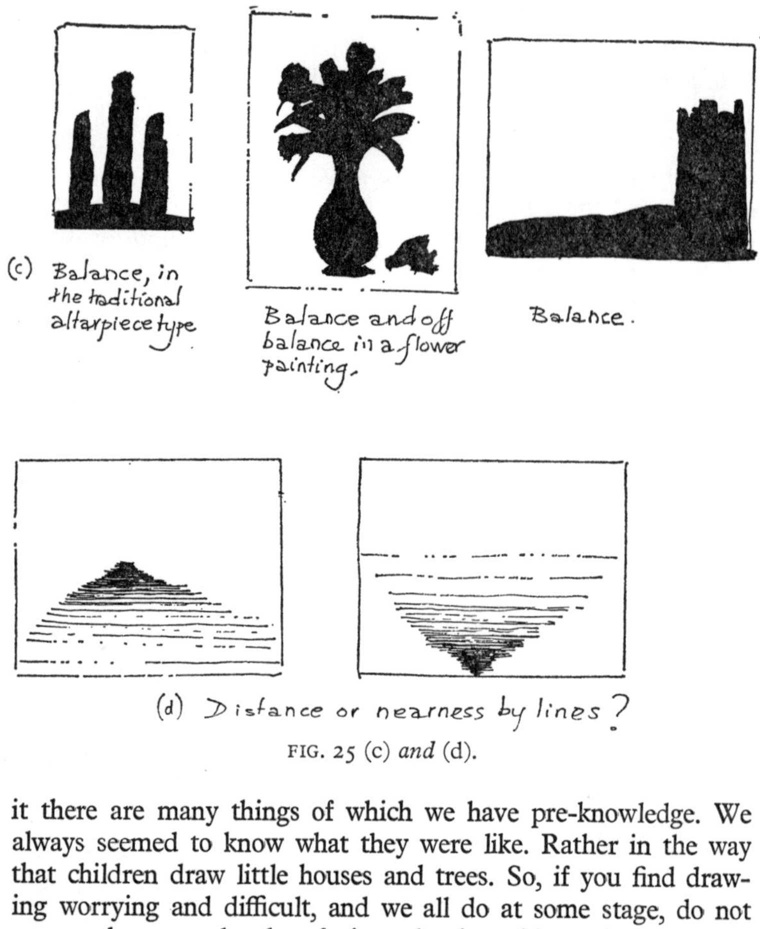

FIG. 25 (c) *and* (d).

it there are many things of which we have pre-knowledge. We always seemed to know what they were like. Rather in the way that children draw little houses and trees. So, if you find drawing worrying and difficult, and we all do at some stage, do not worry, there are bottles, fruit and other things that can take a lot of distortion or simplification without losing their identity. This is the sort of drawing that one can see in cartoons too, where economy of information is very close to humour.

Here goes then. This time you could use tone, lines or anything else. It might, for practice, be a good idea to sketch, not with pencil, but with paint, so that the division between painting and drawing becomes narrower. So, begin with brush and paint and again your rectangles. You will be wondering why so much about rectangles. You can get a composition with the two pieces of card described on page 60, and if the end result is a good composition, fair enough. But the idea of guiding a beginner is

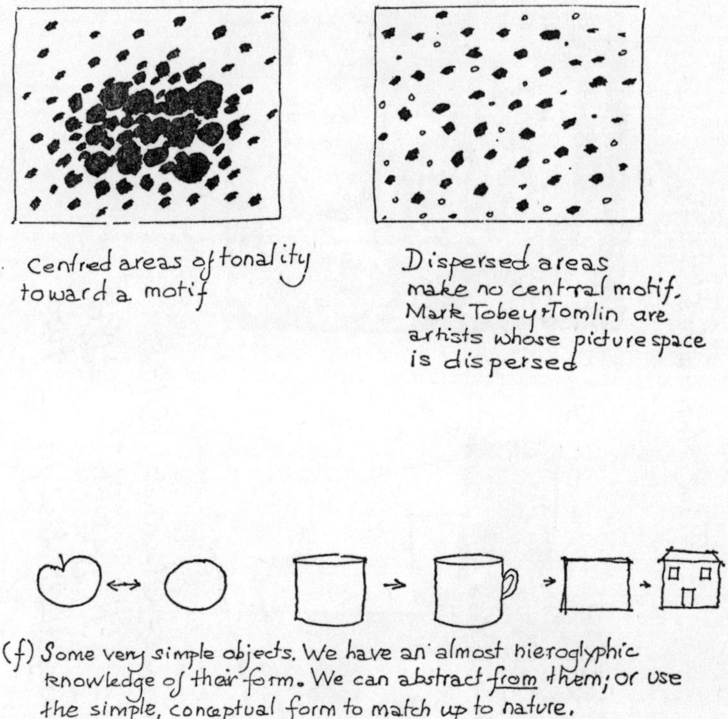

FIG. 25 (e) *and* (f).

to form good habits, it is much better than to start with limitations of the area of the painting and then fitting the shapes into it. Because, at simplest, this is what composition is about, fitting shapes within the area of the picture space. The arrangements within the picture space, or as the rhetoricians of old would say, disposition, is part of the grammar of painting. If you learn a language you can get a fair way by imitation, gesticulation and trial and error, but in the end it is simpler and easier to learn the grammar.

(a) *Now for the familiar objects.* What about a bottle? (See Fig. 26.) Try drawing a bottle in one of the rectangles. Where do you put it? The space that is left out is important too. Put in another bottle, and another, and you have something approaching a still life. Try drawing more bottles still.

(b) For a bit of variation you try the same thing with fruit

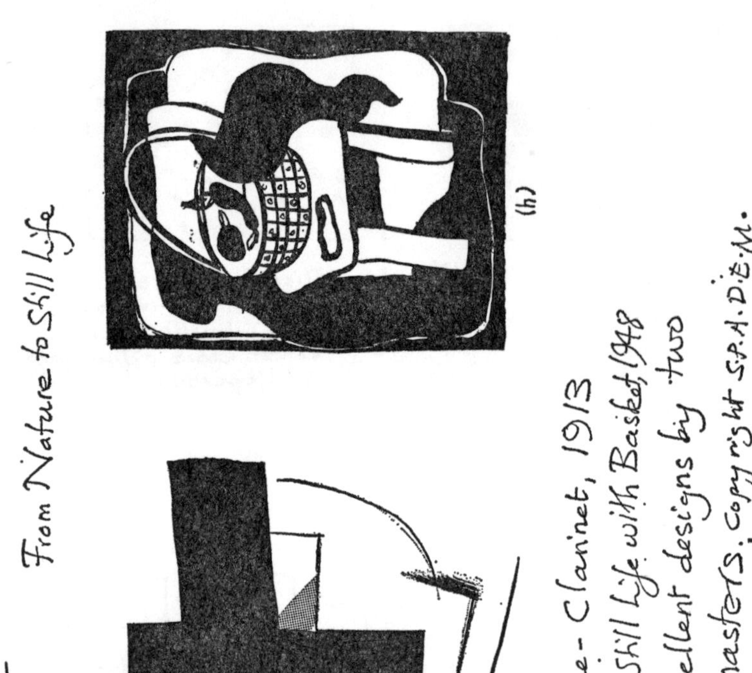

FIG. 25 (g) *and* (n).

(Fig. 27(a)). The drawing 27(b) is taken directly from a painting by Cézanne, very simple, but entirely satisfying. The drawing 27(c) is even simpler and is taken from a Chinese drawing. So you see it does not take much to make a good design.

(c) Looking at cubist paintings you will see jugs, tables, chairs,

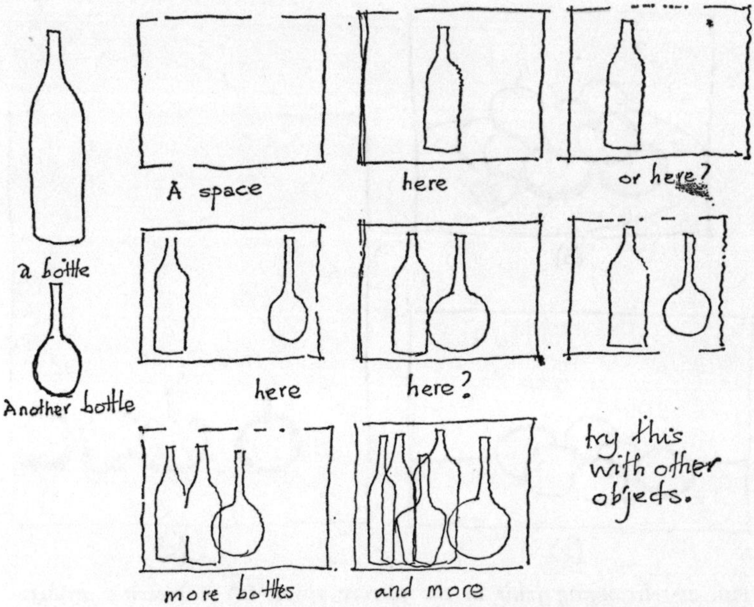

FIG. 26 *Arranging bottles in the picture space.*

etc. These are very good motifs for patterns. You will find you cannot escape the problem of the pattern of the edges. If your drawing does not look right – keep trying. When you draw and paint usually the right idea comes to you by going on drawing. The drawing itself suggests something to you. It is not helpful to get addicted to half-formed images in your head, because the more you are carried away in your imagination, the more the drawing or painting in reality is a disappointment.

(d) Now try a pattern of a composition using several elements you have explored before.

(e) Looking at them, you may find there is one that you would like to turn into a full-scale painting.

(f) As a development from (e) we come to an interesting point. Perhaps one of your drawings makes you want to paint, or draw, further from nature, using your drawing as a model to be compared to nature. This is not unusual in the course of art history. It is what Giotto did when the Byzantine style was his model, and the ancient Greeks must have done the same when they compared stone idols to living beings. In our own lives

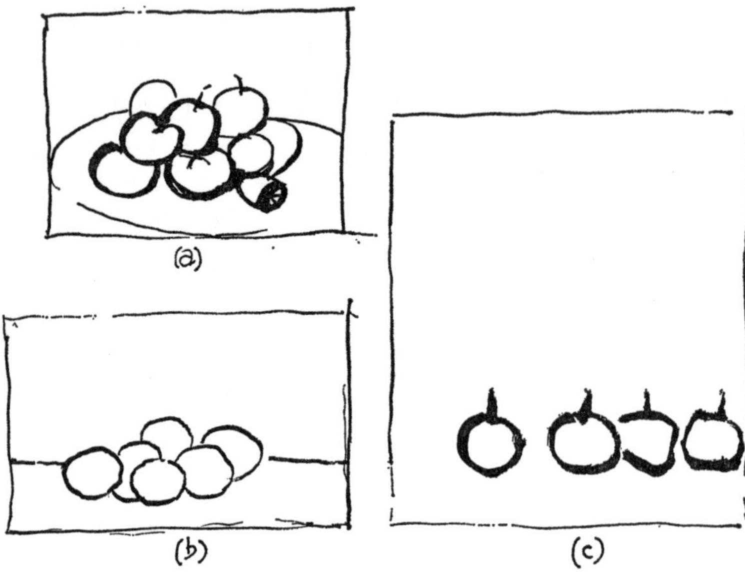

FIG. 27 *Arranging fruit in the picture space.* (a) *A pleasing arrangement.* (b) *A simple design after Cézanne.* (c) *A design taken from a Chinese drawing. Note the differences in the spaces that are left out.*

who does not remember getting very clear characters in our minds from reading books when we were children, then thinking that real people were like them? Something we usually grow out of in life, but very useful in painting.

Basic design in art schools is to teach a fundamental grammar for all the visual arts, and to some extent this has been referred to in the chapter. But, as the prime purpose of the book is about painting, we should come back to this in regard to another aspect of basic design for painters. This is basic design to teach what can be described as a kind of detachment of vision. By detachment of vision is meant looking, really *looking* at an object or group of objects purely in terms of colour and pattern or tone. Most usually, when our eyes look at an object, and remember our eyes are part of our brain, the brain forms words round the object, rather like Proust and his cake. It takes training to be able to concentrate on the objects as shapes. A very good way of doing this is a reversal of the idea expressed on page 74. In effect, drawing directly from the external world, but trying to see the unfamiliar in the obvious. The drawings are to start you off. I hope yours are quite different. Seeing the unfamiliar in the obvious is a way of interpreting the external world so that subjects painted since the beginning of time are always new. Drawing everyday things from unexpected angles will make you see the obvious differently. See the drawings (Figs. 26–28) as

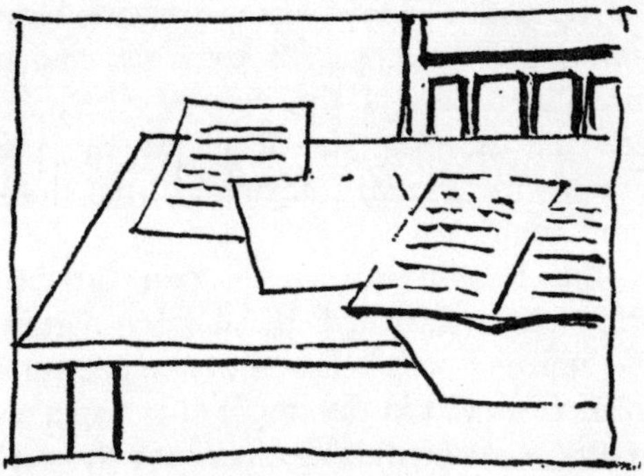

FIG. 28 *An unusual viewpoint.*

they will show you how this can be done at any spare moment.

Many a book on basic design, and there are very good ones about, suggest exercises that are constructions out of yoghurt pots, egg boxes, etc. Please yourself and do them if you like but, if asked, I would say, do not. They are great fun for children, but for a mature person there is something unacceptable in the idea that we can construct art objects out of any old thing. It is an attitude that provokes slovenly workmanship. Throughout the book we will be referring to the Dutch still life painters; these artists' appeal, apart from anything else, is the excellence of their craftsmanship. In your artistic life you may paint many bad paintings, but if the craftsmanship is sound then you have gained something.

This chapter, as others, has classified aspects of design, and referred to grammar. Classification and syntax are methods of organisation. One comes across the idea that you can learn to paint by messing about with paint, or, as educational psychologists put it, experimenting with texture. It is about as possible as being let loose with a piano and without any tuition discover the system of scales. It could happen, but it hasn't yet.

Basic design is an introduction on how to think of problems

that are concerned with the language of things that are seen. It is a way of learning to think in terms of shape, colour, tone, proportion, line, etc. Many a beginner to painting gets into muddles because words about the thing seem to get in the way of the eye-mind and hand. This does not mean only training your eye to painting, but to look for quality in all the natural and man-made creation. A mere altering of a line or a proportion can ruin the whole design. So you can see where basic design is not so different from drawing. All your art studies should train you to sense differences of the greatest degree of refinement in colour, tone and drawing. In effect, training your taste; possibly rather an emasculated word in English, but think of the vigorous French word 'goût'.

Proportion. Once in the Renaissance, proportion attained mystical significance. Proportion mirrored the Divine Order. This was a time when the universe was believed to be geocentric and the motions of the planets moved in the music of the spheres round the earth in a circular movement. The circle was the perfect shape, and according to the only surviving architectural writings of the Romans, those of Vitruvius, the circle measured the proportions of man himself. Modern as we are with our vast cosmological knowledge we can profitably take these ideas into our own scheme of things, even if only to have in our pictures or our surroundings things that are pleasing in proportion. Some artists have an instinct for proportion, but if we feel we have not, the regular solids are a good enough guide. In a practical way proportion can affect the mood of a whole painting. Look at Fig. 29. Have you noticed how many altarpieces are in the shape shown on the left? It is as though the height overpowers us. Think how many landscapes and mythologies are depicted in the longwise (centre) shape, which is static and more serene. Does a square painting have give and take? I happen to think not but you will probably disagree.

Studio Vista have published the classic work on basic design, written by the late Maurice de Sausmarez. Most generously, they have given me permission to quote his excellent definitions of basic design:

'Basic design should be

(a) An attitude of mind, not a method.

(b) Primarily a form of enquiry not a new art form.

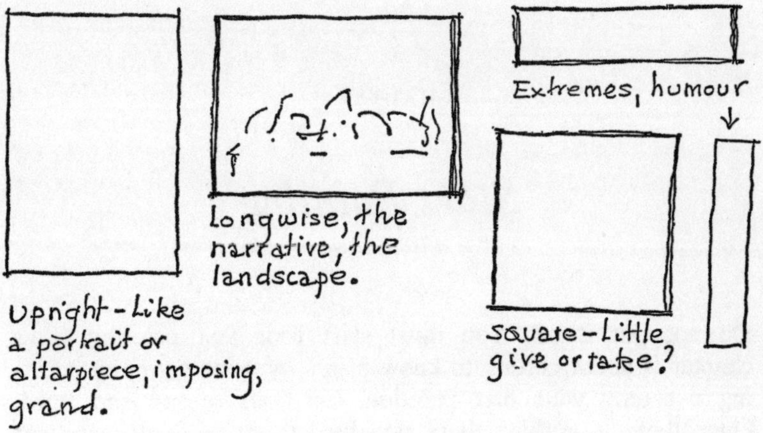

FIG. 29 *Proportions of canvas or boards.*

(c) Not only an enquiry about the marks and structures that appear out of the materials used, but also an enquiry about the sources and terms of personal expression and reactions to the world around us.
(d) Concerned with form in a fundamental sense in every field, it is not exclusively abstract or non figurative; there is as much need for rethinking and reshaping of our attitude to realism and figural studies.
(e) Emphatically not an end in itself but a means of making the individual more acutely aware of the expressive resources at his command; a fostering of inquisitiveness about phenomena, great and small, on the paper or the canvas, in the external world, or the interior world of visions, personal reactions, and preferences.'

CHAPTER 5

Start Painting

Do not put it off. You must start your first painting. This chapter is about getting to know paints by using them, by painting not only your first painting, but your second and third. Once there is a third there will be lots more. Some excellent painting manuals recommend that your first painting should be just playing about with paint. Should this appeal to you there is something about this at the end of the chapter (see page 91). But playing with paint can be a bit like the idea that if you let apes loose on a typewriter eventually they might write like Shakespeare.

What should you paint? You could think about getting to know about white and the earth colours. So, suppose you found some *simple objects in white, buffs, off-whites* and put them on a table. For this first exercise the light should preferably come from the front, without great contrasts of light and shade. Try to have a table you can walk around to find unexpected viewpoints. Before you begin to paint do several drawings as the earlier chapters suggest. Then choose the one you like best to begin your painting.

1. *How to begin.* You have a fair selection of oil paints. There is your palette. Do not squeeze colours on the palette any old how. An orderly palette is important. Now there may be some artists whose genius is so great that it does not matter. There may be, but this is unlikely to be you, or me. Orderly equipment will help raise the ordinary painter to the rather better painter.

There are several ways of setting out a palette (as already referred to in Chapter 2). One is in the colours of the rainbow: white, lemon, mid-yellow, yellow ochre, orange, bright red, dark red, purple, blues, greens, earths, blacks; this also happens to be the tonal grading of the colours. Another is lining the greens, blues, violets opposite the warmer complementaries, red, orange, yellow, with white and earths after this. A third method is grouping the colours to the primary they relate to, a red, lemon and ultramarine. Or invent your own system. So, as you are starting out with only the earth colours set these out. They are white, yellow ochre, light red, raw or burnt umber. Always put out a larger blob of white than all other colours.

2. Now put out your media.

3. Your new white board is facing you. To begin with do not attempt too big a picture, this one should be at greatest length not more than about 40 cm. Yes, boards do face one and try to defend themselves from your approach. But do not let them. Do not be afraid. Before you begin, brushes should be dipped into your medium. Use a small brush now.

4. With very well diluted raw umber outline the main areas of the painting. You *could* outline in charcoal, but I know what will happen if you do, you will get carried away by the drawing and never paint.

5. Now you have an outline there is no going back! Take a large brush, do not be timid, and now decide which is the darkest area. Mix up raw or burnt umber with plenty of medium. It may be tempting to paste paint on but there is a classic rule: *start thin and work up to thicker paint,* that is well worth observing; firstly, for permanence and secondly, thick paint is difficult to work into for a beginner.

6. Rinse the brush you have been using, take another and paint in the white parts. Do not leave the white of the canvas for white in the painting (Fig. 30).

7. Indeed, it is not a good idea to have any bits of white canvas showing through; so next, paint in a sort of medium tone for everything that is neither darkest or lightest. How will you get this medium tone? Perhaps by mixing the white with umber and some ochre. Try a little bit mixed on your palette, if it is not right straightaway add a little of either the white or the umber till it is as nearly right as possible.

8. Rinse brushes and stand back. You have an area filled, and this is the beginning of a painting. You may be in doubt, I suppose one always is when painting; but you may be thinking that Cézanne built up his still lifes in little tiny patches of colour. It is *just* possible that you, as a beginner, could get away with

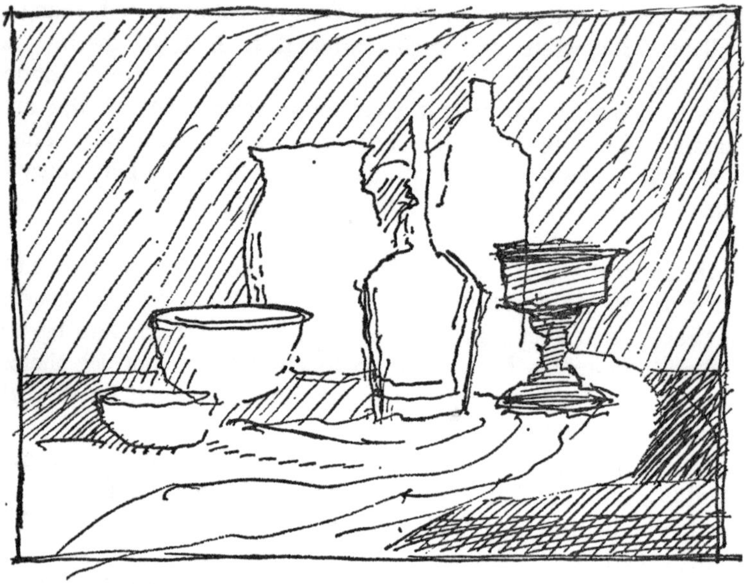

FIG. 30 *When you start painting, be sure to cover* every *area of the board with a thin layer of the approximate colour tone. Try to establish the darkest tone. Equate the lightest with the white on your palette.* Never *think of any area of the painting as less interesting than another.*

this, and try it if you like. But remember Macauley's words, 'Characteristics of style that are most easily copied are the most questionable.' Bad habits are more easily fallen into than good ones are formed.

9. We have to go on. Where to go next? The general pattern of shapes must be made more exact. This is not a matter of getting your smallest sable brush and touching up highlights. This is a major fault of many beginners – it happens to be rather satisfying to do. Do not be tempted to do so, or *do* be tempted, but do not blame me if your paintings get no better. What you should be concentrating on now is building the individual forms. Let us start on one; you can begin by using thicker paint. Paint in large strokes, round the form, down the form (see Fig. 31), using your brush on its tip and side, but do not stipple with the brush as it ruins it. Brushwork is very personal. Some excellent painters' brushwork is not conspicuous, particularly that of many

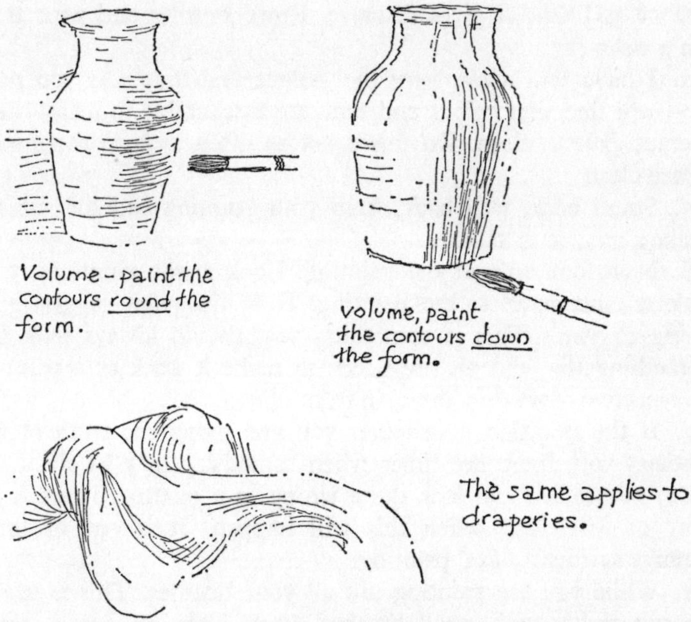

FIG. 31 *Building up form.*

Dutch painters, but others, like Chardin's is.

10. This will bring two more problems. Stand back; your jug may look awkwardly drawn and the rest of the painting may not look right. The rest of the painting may look wrong because if you have concentrated on one bit the rest is out of key.

11. Now as you paint the rest around the jug you have been working on, you will improve the picture and discover another aspect of drawing. Not drawing by line, but drawing by shape. This is a development of what the basic design chapter discussed.

12. You are getting something that looks like a picture. If anything has gone hopelessly wrong here you should scrape out with the palette knife and repaint. When you scrape out with a palette knife you can still see something of the original image to guide you.

13. See that the edges of the painting and the backgrounds are painted to the same degree as every part of the picture. Regarding backgrounds, notice that if yours is painted entirely in one colour it looks like a flat backdrop. If you vary the

colour and tone it gives distance. Rinse brushes and wipe them on a clean rag.

14. I have said above vary the 'colour and tone'. As you paint you will find that colour and tone are inseparable in many cases. Scrape palette clean. Do this every so often to keep the mixing space clean.

15. Stand back, well back, from your painting and the subject. Take a good look at both.

16. Now look only at the painting. Look at the paints on your palette, and again at the painting. Does the paint suggest anything to you? This is something you should always look for, something that the picture needs to make it work as a painting irrespective of what is 'there' in front of you.

17. If the question of whether you are giving the truth or not bothers you, there are times when something may be the truth from nature but can look quite wrong in a picture. There is no way of foretelling when this will happen. It is one of those strange accidents of oil painting.

18. While you are painting use all your brushes. This is to say do not tinker with small brushes, learn large, sweeping movements. Tinkering with small brushes is a common fault of most beginners.

19. Mistakes. Just in case things are looking awful. No guide in the world can show you how not to make them. Bad paintings are bound to happen. Accept this and accept too that you can get depressed. The only cure is to do another painting. Perhaps it is more painful for the artist to bear that despite the striving the product of one's agony will be mediocrity. You might as well learn too, and learn early, that the best paintings come from steady, even dull, work. Moments of intense inspiration happen very seldom; and if they happen at all probably end in disappointment.

20. Turn the picture upside down. You should do this quite regularly as this makes mistakes show up that you would not otherwise have noticed.

21. You have to repaint again. Never be afraid of drastically altering a painting. You will probably find that when you have altered one part of the picture it will bring out good and bad things in other parts.

22. How long should you go on with this painting? Let us say

six sessions of about an hour and a half each session or a little longer. Painters, whether beginners or experienced, should keep a balance between paintings that are taken as far as possible, and ones that are left when you have achieved a quick lively effect. It is pleasing to get quick effects, but dangerous to rely on them the whole time.

23. As you get to know the tactile quality of your colours and board, you will become increasingly aware that there comes a point when you no longer feel excited by working into the paint. Then a picture is finished.

You know the earth colours by now and, like learning a language, colours are your vocabulary and you increase this vocabulary as you go on. Vocabulary becomes reasoned speech through grammar and the next exercise in the grammar of painting is tonality. Tonality, by definition in the *Oxford Dictionary* is: 'The degree of luminosity in a colour.' Tonality is measured between black and white. Suppose we tried exercises in these colours separately, and then together. You need not use black on your palette and many painters do not. But no oil painter can do without white.

1. Try to set up a white still life with as many white things as you can find.

2. Put out a large amount of both titanium and flake white on your palette. If you compare the oil paint, as it is, to the whites in the still life you will notice the great variety of hints of other colours that white contains, so you will need a little of almost every other colour.

3. Do not be tempted to leave tracks of bare canvas or you will not get much out of the exercise.

4. Do a preliminary sketch on paper and put the main outlines which should be transferred to your board. Even for the merest exercise use a well-prepared board. There is no reason why something begun as an exercise should not become a work of art.

5. Look very carefully at the still life. How much of what you see compares to the titanium white that is on your palette? Possibly not as much as you think. But for what there is, paint it on fairly thinly, with your paint mixed with medium. The titanium white will be even lighter than most white primings. Here now you have your absolute white; the whitest white on

the palette which equates to the brightest white you can see.
6. Try to mix the white that is furthest from this absolute white.
7. You will discover that with the merest hint of another colour white loses its purity and is reduced in tonality.
8. Now paint the other colours of white, including the darks of the shadows.
9. If the end result looks patchy you can now explore flake white. But first the painting should be allowed to dry for a few days.
10. With flake white *well* diluted paint all over the picture in a scumble till you have a unity of colour.
11. Go on painting in flake white and the other colours if you like the idea of painting thicker with flake white. If you like white paintings try others.

Black and darks. Black is the other extreme. You could either set up a still life using black and very dark colours, or for a change, why not try an abstract? You should try any size of painting you like.
1. Paint a wide stripe of black. This does not have to be a stripe, it could be a square, but just as long as you can see clearly the colours you are putting on.
2. Now you can see the extreme of contrast between the black paint and the white of the board. Rinse brushes.
3. Look very carefully. What colour on the palette is nearest in depth to the black? On a single palette it may be the raw umber; though if you have many colours it may be the pthalocyanine colours. Paint this in a stripe next to the black as shown in Fig. 32.
4. Then paint in stripes of the next dark range of colours, which are likely enough to be the ultramarine and crimson.
5. Look very carefully again to assess how much darker black is compared to the other colours.
6. Give each stripe another coat of its colour to be sure that the board is well covered and there are no white bits showing through.
7. See if the other darks are transparent compared to the black. The black may have gone dense or dull, showing that if you are using black extensively you will have to use some varnish and medium.

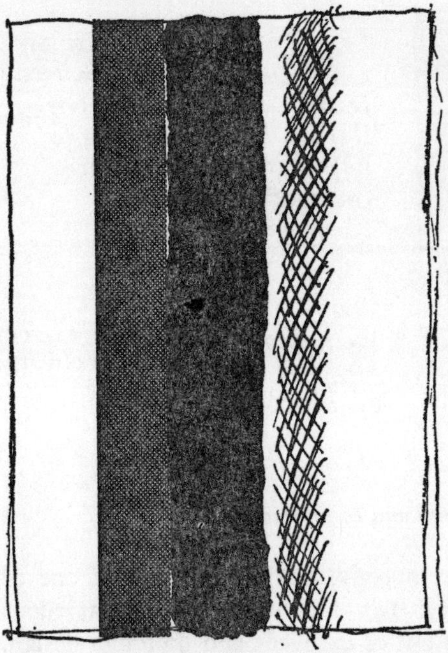

FIG. 32 *You cannot get darker than black. How near do the darkest colours get to black?*

8. Now mix some white with the colours you have used. Paint a stripe of each, white and black over black, ultra and white over ultra, till you have completed the area of the board.
9. Look at the contrast in character of darks alone and darks mixed with white. It shows you that the tendency of darks is to be transparent, and that colours mixed with white are opaque. This is a key factor in painting darks or shadows in oil paint. If, by accident, a dark has gone muddy through too much white in the mixture the cure is to wait until it is dry and then glaze. The glaze should be a dark colour without any white in it at all. This is a general rule and useful for whatever you are painting, but particularly in flesh colour.

By the extremes of black and white you establish the tonality of other colours. Another useful exercise is translating colours into their tonal equivalents of black, white and grey. This is particularly useful to effect distance and recession as well as pattern. A very good way of studying both these is to copy colour reproductions of paintings. For an example to copy tone to effect distance, a landscape painting is very useful. Please

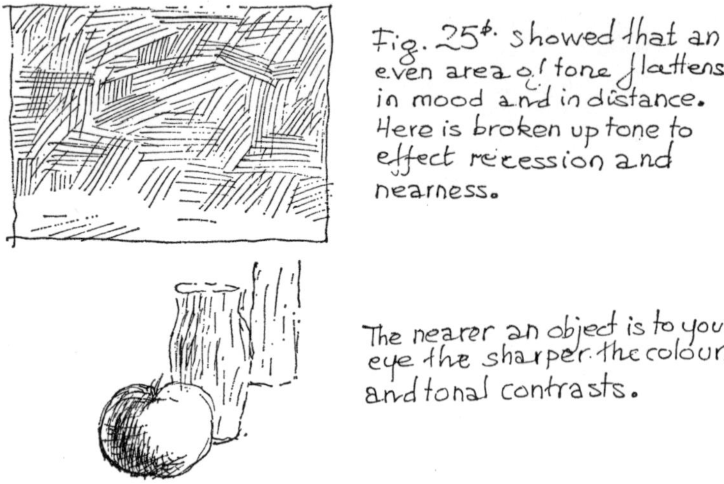

FIG. 33 *Even and contrasted tone.*

yourself what you choose to copy, but I have chosen one of Claude Lorraine's (see Fig. 14). Not only is it a marvellous example of tonal recession but of excellent and thorough design. Broken-up tone can also be used to effect recession and nearness (see Fig. 33). For pattern in tones of colour you could copy a Matisse or a Mondrian.

From the first two exercises in this chapter you will have noticed that tonality creates solid form. There is yet another aspect of tonality, the drama of light and shade. None of these definitions of the use of tone in painting is mutually exclusive, but to divide them makes them more easily recognised.

Tone the drama of light and shade. In this exercise you could add ultramarine, lemon and red to your palette.

1. Set up a still life where you can see strong contrast of light and shade. Set up any kind of still life, with more objects and a few more colours than before. Fig. 34 gives an example.

2. Do some preliminary drawings, not just outline, but tonal, so that you can work out balance of light and shade.

3. Start to work on the painting as soon as possible. First, in the very lightest and darkest areas. Try at this stage, to keep whites out of the shadows. If possible, use different sets of brushes for the darks and the lights.

4. Try to paint the shadows, using mixtures with ultramarine

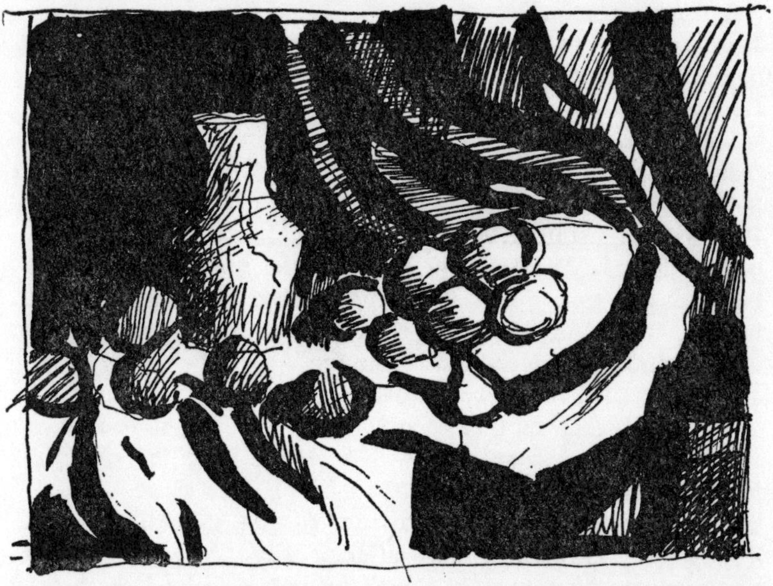

FIG. 34 *Here the subject is strongly lit from one angle to effect the sharpest possible contrast between light and shade. Tone as light and dark is more important than tone as colour.*

and some black. Notice how you will get cold shadows. You can get a neutral, rather dense shadow by mixing ultramarine and light red.

5. The painting is now sharply divided between light and dark. Look very carefully. Have the darks no colour, or do you see colours in shadows? Paint them in if you do.

6. Then there are the middle-toned colours. Making a mixed colour is a matter of taking the colour (with the tip of your brush) on the palette which is nearest to the colour you are looking at, and then, if there is something of another colour, take a little of that. Mix them with medium on the centre of your palette. Does it still need another colour? Maybe, but always try to get mixtures with as few colours as possible. The mixture may be too dark, so add a little white. If it is too light, take care about adding black, raw umber is a gentler way of making darks. Naturally you will not get anything exact, but a near approximation.

7. How does a bright colour equate in tonality to dark shadows

and bright light? This puzzles the most experienced painters. A way of seeing a tone is to half shut your eyes. A bright, near object has greater intensity than a further shadow. As colour recedes from the eye it loses its intensity. So paint the bright colour. Do not forget to stand well back as you are working, so that you always see the painting as a whole. Rinse brushes!

8. Do not depend on me all the time to tell you what to do. Paint as your instinct tells you.

9. Stand back. Perhaps you have painted something that you believed was true, yet it was wrong in the painting. This can happen. There are a number of truths: your own vision, what is there, and what 'works' in the painting.

10. It is a good rule never to overwork one part of the painting at the expense of another. What usually happens, if you do, is that you have to scrape out with a palette knife the part you have concentrated on. So keep the *whole* picture going.

11. As you paint remember to use, at first, all your brushes. Try putting the paint on in different ways. Also, try holding the brush in different ways. One's instinct is to hold the brush like a pen, but if you hold it in your fist you develop a broader approach. If, at first, you use every kind of brush you get to know what your favourites are. Most artists, like any craftsmen, have their favourite tools. If you find you have favourite brushes it is a taste you should indulge in. Do not forget to rinse them and wipe them as you go.

12. You have a lemon yellow on your palette, do not forget to use this as a lightener of darks; you will get some quite unusual colours.

13. We are studying light and shade as balance and as the creator of solid form. Looking into the shadows you will see that there are colours, hot and cold. While you cannot separate tone and colour, it is a question of bias. That is to say, some shadows are simply greys, browns and blacks, and in others you can see more colours. A strongly lighted subject is biased to light and shade. Study again the balance. Has the painting too even a balance? Should some light or dark be altered to make the picture look more exciting? For, you may have found, that however much you plan a painting in a drawing, the actual painting on the board may upset the plans; it does not always but it can sometimes. This is one of the adventures of painting

in oils, the element of the unpredictable. And, indeed, if what was planned is not to your liking you can change it.

14. Next look for dark and light for extension in depth. You have the table top, that takes you into the depth of the picture space, but also consider how the light and dark does. Look again for a point made earlier about the nearer you are to an object the sharper will be the contrast. Look again to see if distances diminish the intensity of shadows. If you were to paint a background quite black it would not make for a depth of darkness, it would flatten it.

15. The drama of light and shade is not something that at the time of writing is particularly fashionable for the painter, nor has it been for about a hundred years. But fashion does not mean that you should not try something. As a painter never be worried by what is in the fashion. The artist makes the fashion, not the fashion the artist.

16. The important rule about light and shadow is that of consistency. That is, you have to be consistent about the source of light. If light comes from a variety of sources you get into a hopeless muddle.

17. Painting in terms of light and dark is particularly associated with the seventeenth-century baroque. You should study seventeenth-century paintings of every subject to see some really beautiful examples. You will find that most paintings are lit from the side or the front. This should not prevent you from making experiments in lighting from other directions.

To return to where we started; on page 80. To think of learning painting as a musician learns keys in scales may not appeal to you. So here, as promised, is the idea of the other extreme of starting with messing about and seeing what will happen. If asked, I would say it is a thoroughly bad idea, but this is about *your* work. You may like the end result in the same way as a doting campus mum hearing her offspring banging on the piano thinks that he has discovered tonal music. If you are thinking of the greatest of all abstract painters and expressionists, the action painter, Jackson Pollock, remember he arrived at his unique method after a long traditional training. So here you go.

Put on any colour you please in any shape you like, then choose another colour to contrast and so build up your picture.

In this sort of painting there is no reference to external nature. All you refer to is the paint and board and their demands. After a while you will find that painting by feel and apparent instinct is not all that easy. The instinct is only apparent, for you will always find yourself standing back to question and calculate what colour or shape goes with one or another. If you paint from things in the external world these give your paintings a code of reference for the onlooker. Painting from paint gives none. Therefore, in relation to other people the language of criticism is not whether your painting looks like something. Many people looking at abstract painting expect to find in it more than it contains. It is a question of whether the colours, tones, shapes and textures appeal to the onlooker. To return to painting and once more to Jackson Pollock (see Fig. 35). By his own account it appears that he hypnotised himself into a frenzy of activity while flinging the paint on the canvas. Only

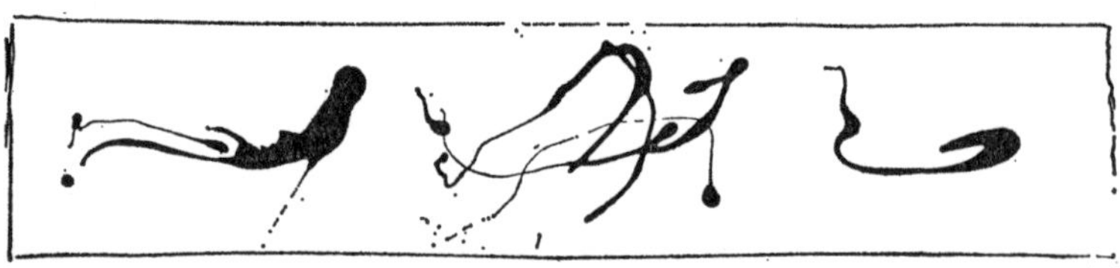

FIG. 35 *Jackson Pollock painting, 1950. Look too at the shapes he leaves out!*

when this frenzy subsided did he stand back to look at what he had done. This is a good idea, if you can do it, to let everything go and just paint. But you cannot extend beyond the confines of the board. This way of painting seems so easy that we may wonder that there are not many more action painters of merit. We may ask too, why there are not more paintings of lines and squares like Mondrian's. The answer is, that we cannot escape the basic laws of painting. You will have learned too of the approaches to abstractions. The one, in basic design, where the picture space was always ordered. The other, which we have just looked at, where you begin with chaos and go on with chaos, hoping it has its own coherence, if not rules. If asked to decide for a beginner which is the best approach, I should say, without hesitation, order.

Clean your equipment!

From Alberti, Florentine architect, theorist, papal secretary and athlete, writing in 1435:

'But as experts hold, I would have all the highest industry and skill in knowing how to use black and white, it is well to take all pains and care in knowing how to use these two well, for light and shade make things seem to be in relief.'

From Vincent Van Gogh, Dutch-French painter, writing in 1886:

'I am going to use black and white boldly on my palette just as they are . . . they are colours with simultaneous contrasts as striking as that of red and green.'

CHAPTER 6

The Formal Still Life and More About Colour

Alberti, the Florentine humanist, papal secretary and first theoretical writer on sculpture, architecture and painting since antique times, wrote in 1436:

'Since painting strives to represent things seen, let us note in what way things are seen. First in seeing a thing we say it occupies a place. Here the painter in describing this space, will say this, his guiding his outline with a line, is circumscription. Then, looking at it again we understand that several planes of the observed body belong together, and here the painter drawing them in their places will say he is making a composition. Finally, we determine more clearly the colours and qualities of the planes, since every difference in them is born from light, we can properly call their representation the reception of light.'

Alberti goes on to give an excellent definition of composition: 'Composition is that rule of painting by which those parts of the things seen fit together in the painting.'

Can composition have formal rules? In this chapter I am assuming that there can be formal rules, though there are always painters whose pictures hang together by an internal logic of their own. This borders on the aspects of painting that cannot be taught. The purpose of this chapter is to assume that there are formal laws that can be taught, in the same way that an academy of music has a teacher of composition. In fact we are ordering experience within an art form. The great figure compositions of the past, which the theories of Alberti did so much to form, were of epic subjects from human life, yet beyond human life. The deliberate and conscious gesture of the figures in a Raphael composition are no more about ordinary life than is the Aeneid. They are recreations of life on a higher, more ordered plane. It is not surprising that until recent times this sort of composition was always set to students as the most exacting test of their ability. It is a curious fact that this was abandoned as being exacting but pointless, yet one has not seen art students become better artists for never having been trained in composition. The still life then is a helpful way of studying composition, without having the feeling of painting something that bears no relation to everyday life. For Cézanne the still life was the means by which he put into practice his statements that he wished 'To redo Poussin after nature', and to 'Make impressionism as solid and enduring as the art in the galleries.'

As well as more elaborate and formal compositions we will also be concerned with increasing your colour range and getting to know more of the colours on the artists' palette.

The still lifes set as examples below are all based on classic forms of compositions. A classic form can stand up to any mount of reinterpretation.

The first (Fig. 36) is based on one of the many beautiful

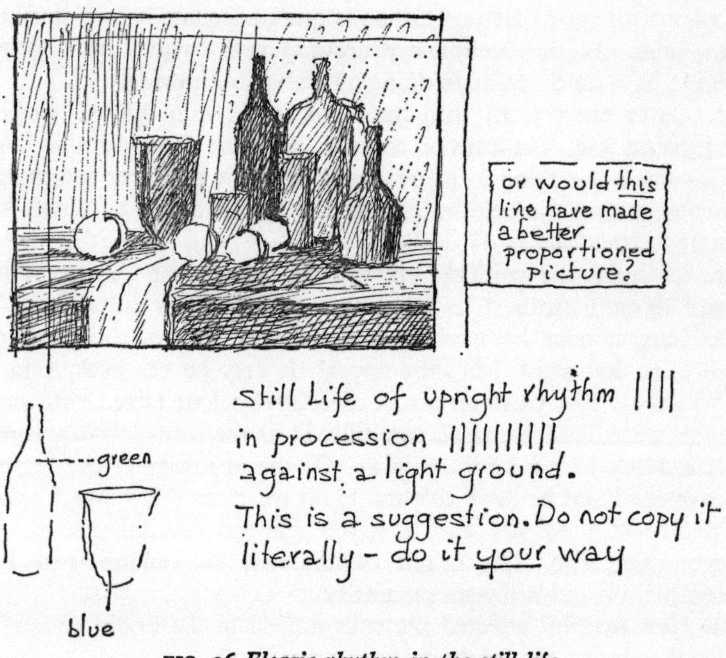

FIG. 36 *Elegaic rhythm in the still life.*

examples of still lifes painted by Chardin, though you should make the same experiment in your own way using a still life of your choice. It has been chosen for its solemn, elegaic rhythm. The drawing shows a few more colours and a light ground. Other compositions in the solemn elegaic rhythm are Piero della Francesca's fresco *The Arrival of the Queen of Sheba,* and a more modern example is Courbet's oil painting *Burial at Ornans*. The rhythm is effected by the upright rows of forms in all cases.

To paint. Colours should be arranged on your palette, your board should be about the size of your forearm length longways and about half that in height. When, as might be advisable, you do your preliminary drawings, you should vary the proportions of the shape of the composition to see if this affects the mood. In any case the board you paint on should not be so small that it's a miniature, nor so large that it frightens you. Copy the preliminary drawing on to your board. You can either 'square up' or draw by free-hand. You can draw on the board in charcoal or use a thin brush and a thin dilution of any of the colours on your palette. Outline is quite adequate before starting to paint. As the preliminary drawing gets covered with paint there isn't much point in doing an elaborate drawing.

1. Cover main areas with main colours in thin diluted washes of paint. Get the canvas covered, and use large brushes. At this stage the thing is to get going and not to worry too much about getting the colours exactly right. There will be plenty of time for this later.

2. To build the painting up, you can start using thicker paint and thinner brushes. In painting a still life it is quite sensible to start at once by working into the very part of the painting that, at first sight, has *least* appeal. It may be the background. You could just paste on a sort of neutral colour mixed with raw umber and blue. But look carefully. Does the neutral background reflect any of the bright colours? Or the opposites of the bright colours? Paint in these colours if you see them. Now stand back.

3. One area painted and now you will see that this shows up everything else. The bright colours may be looking weak by comparison and will want repainting.

4. How has this affected the colours next to the bright colours? Do they reflect the bright colours in any way?

5. All the painting area should be built up now.

6. Stand back, always stand back as you work. It makes you see the good bits you may have painted by accident.

7. Are some of the background objects jumping out at you? Maybe there is no recession. This could be because there is too much sharp outline of the object against the background. You know that there must be a boundary yet painting one may not look right in terms of the painting itself. With a dry brush rub the edge of the object into the background, and you may find you have effected recession.

8. Perhaps the coloured objects are looking flat. You know quite well by now that you model solid form by adding darks. This though is to miss out all the discoveries of colour of the impressionists and their followers. Are the shadows just dark? Or do you see the opposite colours? Are shadows as vivid as lights or do you see in shadows loss of colour as light is lost? These are but suggestions, and at all times you must paint what you see.

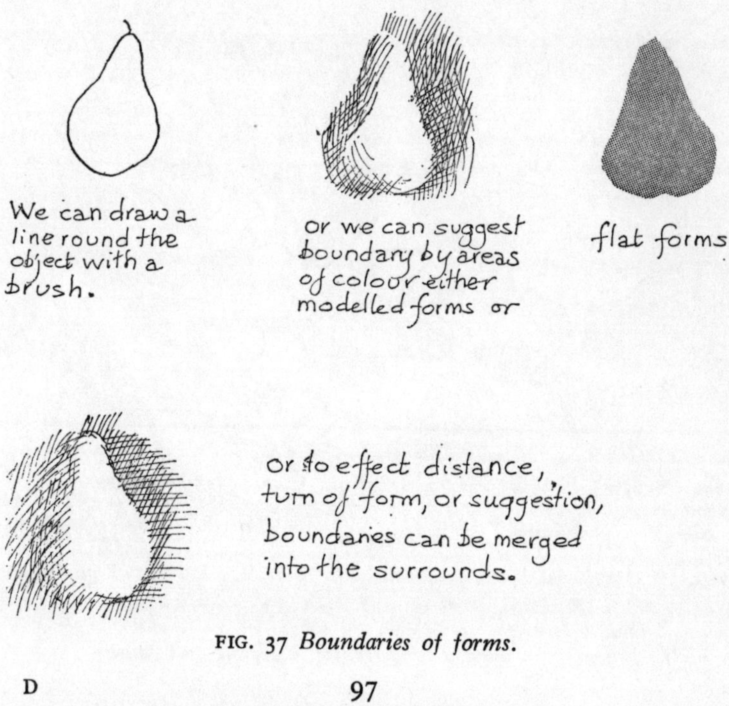

FIG. 37 *Boundaries of forms.*

9. Be sure you have not left one bit or corner unpainted that is distracting the rest of the painting.

10. Consider this interesting case of boundary again. Do you see some merged and others clear. Fig. 37 gives some suggestions.

11. All the while you paint, be self critical. Could you vary the brush marks to make the paint surface more interesting?

12. Should you move around the paint to effect the suggestion of form that you read from a distance, rather than fully delineate?

13. Always remember that when you get something that goes wrong the cure may lie in drastic alteration or repainting what is next to it.

14. Remember too that the above exercise is an extension of the previous chapter.

15. And that the very bit you have most enjoyed painting may, alas, be the bit that distracts the rest, and will have to be removed by palette knife.

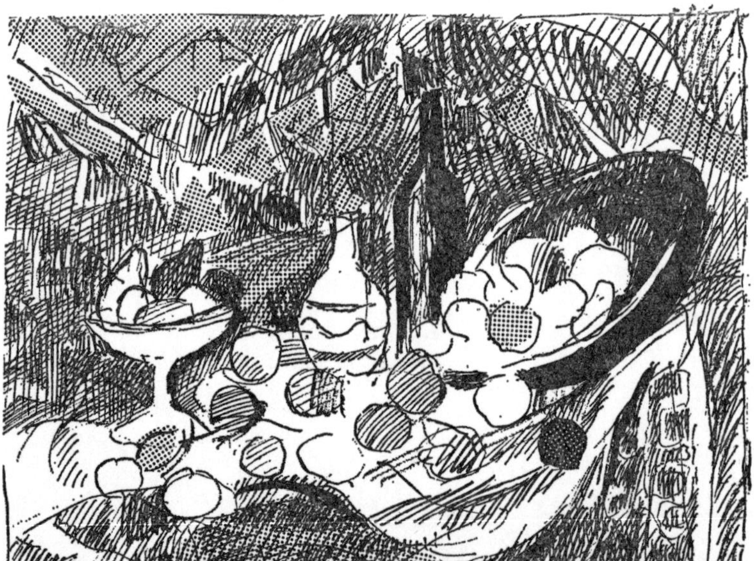

FIG. 38 *A schema based on a still life in rich colours and movement. Suggestions for fruit – orange and rich reds. Suggestions for background and draperies – rich patterned fabric in blues and purples. The schema is a variant of de Heem, Cézanne and Matisse.*

16. Don't forget to turn pictures upside down. This shows up some startling things.

The next still life is all together more elaborate in composition and colour. In this one we look at Bacchic-Dionysiac rhythm associated with richness and splendour. The picture (Fig. 38) is based on a still life by de Heem (see page 173). This still life was copied by Matisse directly, and indirectly in reverse by Cézanne. It is not difficult to see why. The design has rhythm, rich tonality and variety in form. One is led to speculate whether de Heem himself could have seen, in Antwerp, some of the grand compositions of Rubens. There can be no better examples of Old Master paintings in Bacchic rhythm than those by Titian painted in the 1520s for the studiolo of Alphonso D'Este of Ferrara. These were indeed of the myths of Bacchus, all of great beauty and splendour. Perhaps the finest composition in complexity of rhythm and design, drawing and colour is *Bacchus and Ariadne* in the National Gallery, London. In ecstatic rhythm too is Poussin's *Worship of the Golden Calf*, also in the National Gallery, painted over a hundred years after Titian's.

To compare then the still life, the idea is to take the drawing to start you off. Every person will take a different arrangement of more or less the same basic material. The idea is really to enjoy yourself with the richest colour fruits and draperies. If rhythm creates mood so does colour. Use colour to express all that you feel about splendour and grandeur. Walk around the still life. It will show up all kinds of new faces you did not notice (Fig. 39).

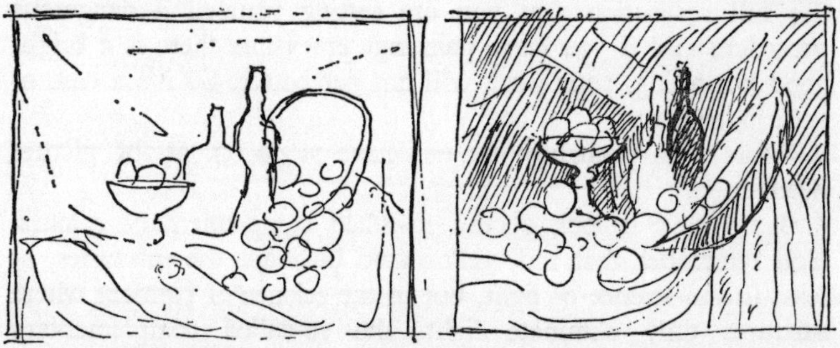

FIG. 39 *Walk round any still like you have arranged. You will find new faces and different compositions.*

To paint. Put out as many colours as you please, but please, to get to know them, include orange, purple and even another green, as well as any others that you like – a full palette.

1. The English painter, Matthew Smith, who painted some very good still lifes once said that a picture is finished before it is begun. Smith was an oil painter but he is expressing an old and traditional attitude by saying that you have to be certain in your mind of the final image. In a way, you do, but there always may come a time when the painting itself must have its way, and for the sake of a good painting you have to change plan.

2. When you look at an area of colour, say a blue in the background, you often see a variety of colours within the one definition. This does not mean that at first you should try putting all the colours on at once, as this may get you into an unholy muddle. So, as always, cover the whole area of the board with the main colours. You may be thinking of Cézanne who used tiny strokes of paint applied with a sable brush, only bit by bit eliminating the white area of the canvas. If you would rather try this way go ahead, but as a beginner you may find the white area of the canvas distracting.

3. You may find that the board or canvas looks perfectly good with just the first layer of painted colour, clear direct and flat. Well! This can and does happen and it is quite obvious that Matisse may have painted many of his lively and delightful still lifes as 'one offs'. If you really feel you have something spontaneous and jolly good, don't be puritanical and go on for the sake of it, out of a misplaced sense of duty. Leave it. But, with the full realisation that you are setting yourself a dangerous precedent and if you leave paintings *everytime* there is a bright good beginning, your work will not get better. So it's a case of your judgement.

4. More than probably you will have to go on, as the picture needs it.

5. Let's have a look at the so-called complementary colours. You remember that red, yellow and blue are the primaries, at least in the science of light, but in the science of pigment where mixtures only eliminate light, the so-called complementary colours have every claim to be primary. Take a look at orange. Paint some on to red and it makes red hotter. Paint some fruit

orange. Compare the clarity of real orange with a mixture of yellow and red, which is only the shadow of orange, and should be used for modelling form only. Then a real purple, perhaps a mineral violet, a precious colour. See the soft neutral beauty of a real purple. Use it to soften blues and darken the turn on yellow forms.

6. Take a look at reds and yellows. Are they really hot colours? Think of the beautiful clothes that Velazquez painted; to him red was always a cool colour. How can one make red cool? A hint of white or even black? A touch of the complementary in the red, makes for neutrality, but not for coolness. Crimson lake is probably the hottest red, and the quinacridone pink the coldest.

7. In the same way, look at blue. Are blues always cold and remote, making for distance, or are they warm and rich with addition of some red?

8. Is the painting looking patchy? In itself this need not be harmful. But what may be distracting is disparity of tones. Always remember that every colour has its comparative tone.

9. If a colour looks wrong, check the tonal colour of the one next to it.

10. As you paint, change as you go from thin to thicker brushes, and don't forget to keep rinsing and wiping brushes. Every so

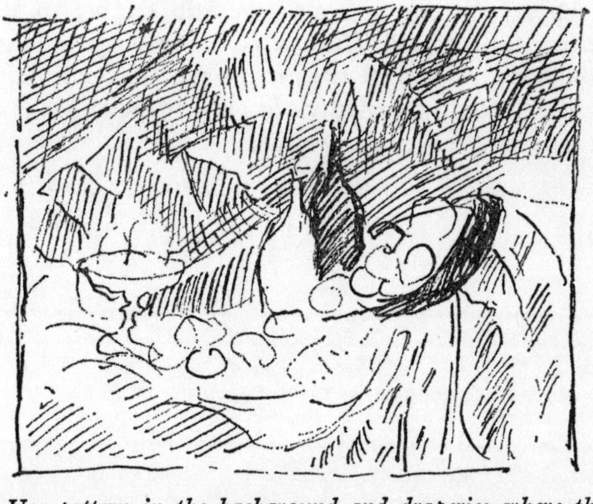

FIG. 40 *Use pattern in the background and draperies where they help the composition. Merge them indefinitely if they are distracting.*

often think of painting the broad masses with marks with a small brush, and the details with a large brush.

11. The illustration (Fig. 40) shows a patterned background. How much pattern should you show? I suggest using it where it helps the composition, but not where bits of it distract your eye from the whole.

12. The drawing may be sound, the basic composition may be hanging together, but there is disunity.

13. You could be really drastic, and scrape down with a palette knife. This will merge the colours, giving that elusive quality, the colour of the air. This means the pervading atmosphere of colour that unifies a picture space; you could be even more drastic and wipe off with a rag.

14. There is no hurry over a still life that does not contain flowers, so you could let the painting grow gradually, using slow techniques like glazing (see page 158).

15. Think broadly, do not think that finishing a picture is adding little bits at the end. Finishing is not like decorating a cake. As you paint try not to separate detail from mass. Think and look at a single apple, are its rosy cheeks something that you add on, or are they part of its surface? Think of the pattern on the jug. It is not something you add for fun, it is describing the circumference of the whole (Fig. 41).

The above two approaches to the still life are to start you off to think for yourself. There is no reason why an elegaic still life should not be in rich colours, or the Bacchic in shades of white. We certainly use flowers in our everyday life to express

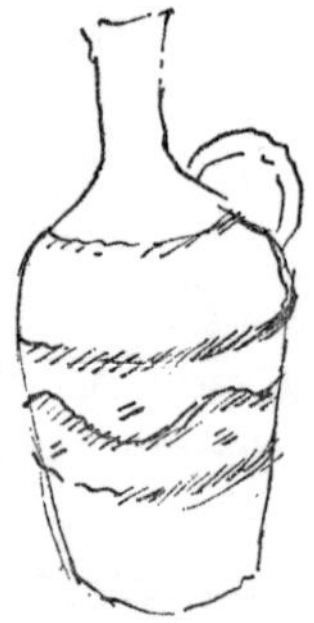

FIG. 41 *Patterns on individual objects explain the turn of forms and may help the whole composition.*

our moods and this is a possibility in a still life as composition too. All the illustrations in the book are only to get you going, to give you the barest skeleton on which to put the flesh and blood of your own personality as an artist.

Before going on to yet another example, I shall divert a bit. The distinguished Royal Academician and Professor, Carel Weight, described his attitude to painting as adventure that took him where he knew not, he often had no distinct plan. This in fact does not contradict Matthew Smith quoted earlier. Painting is often about contradictions in the same way way that we as persons contain contradictions and opposites. You may be the sort to whom a canon of classical rules could never apply, your work has its own unity. Rules may put you off. You may like, in still life, to put in any old thing, any old how, taking something else out of the painting, and so it will go on. For you the classic systems of scale and proportion have no meaning, only your inner vision has meaning. So let's divert to painters whose inner vision is more real than the external world. I imagine that, to these sort of painters, their inner vision expresses itself through visual symbols taken from the external world. While it's difficult to think of a still life painter, one can certainly think of Odilon Redon's beautiful flower paintings or Samuel Palmer's landscape drawings. But both these artists were deeply aware of the care and respect of their materials, the one set of rules that apply to us all. Painting from the inner vision has often been put together with primitive art. The one thing they have in common is, unlike learning rules of order, you cannot decide to be a visionary painter any more than trying to be a primitive or a child artist, you are or you are not. This is not the same as surrealism which is dealt with on another page.

We ought to be getting back to the problems of still life as composition. This time . . .

Still life as landscape. 'Poussin after nature,' as Cézanne said. Let us remember Poussin's beautiful and ordered landscapes. Here (Fig. 42(a)) is a still life from a classical pattern, derived from Chardin and Cézanne again. The mass to one side a reminder of Poussin's device, and the diagonals too take you in and to the distance. We shall also be exploring some green.

Arrange the still life, some fine flowers with leaves in a nice jug, some drapery undulating into the distance. What colour

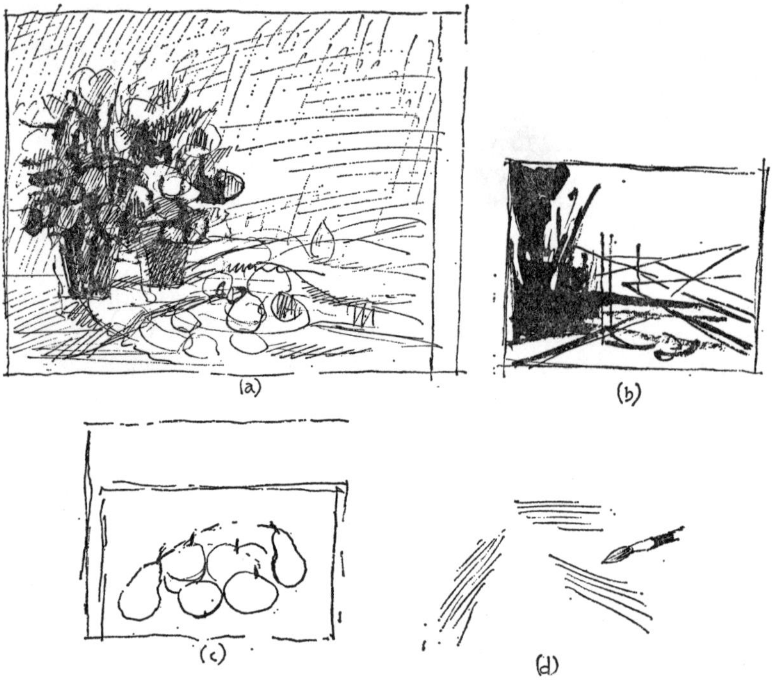

FIG. 42 (a) *Still life as landscape. Suggestions – many rich greens in fruit and plants, pale grey-green in background, white draperies.* (b) *Dark masses to one side, diagonals leading into picture; schema based on Poussin's* Diogenes Throwing Away His Bowl. (c) *An example that the detail is the* all. *The stalks on the fruit unify the picture.* (d) *Try using brush strokes to effect recession and distance.*

background? Red is too frontal and forward to effect landscape, blue we have already looked at as the colour to set off rich reds and yellows. Some more green, we could try that.

1. For your palette, maybe some more greens, emerald and monestial and the brilliant cadmium pale green if you feel extravagant.

2. Look for a moment at the greens. The greens on your palette are all cold. This is a basic charactistic of greens, with the exception of terre vert which never stands up to being mixed anyway. Even in some ways greens are inclined to be neutral.

3. Your painting. It does not have to be too big again. But get started.

4. Main areas again. Remember that the white in the still life has to equate to the white on your palette. All other tones and colours have to be related to this. A fact that is not only useful in the still life but continually useful in landscape and portrait. However brilliantly sun may glisten on water, white on your palette is its tonal equivalent. In a portrait one is always amazed at how much darker than this very fair skins are. So in your painting and this still life in particular, keep looking back to white as the key to all the colour tones. Indeed there are many painters who insist on having white in their paintings so as always to have a key of comparison.

5. Greens. Unless you have chosen a particularly vivid emerald for the background, it is very unlikely that any green in plant and vegetable life will match the green on your palette. The greens of nature are warm. There are many ways of making greens warm and these are basically by mixing the green on the palette with any of the warm colours. Yellows keep greens tonally at their highest pitch, reds will turn green to a warm brown, orange will turn any green to a rich khaki.

6. Try mixing the greens on the palette with blue. They become very cold. Paint some on the background and on the turn of the leaves. Do you find this gives the picture recession? Are cold colours in general nearer or more distant, or do warm colours bring things closer?

7. Can the way you put on brush strokes create the effect of things going away? Try this.

8. Does white lose its intensity as it recedes from the eye? How can you make white lose its intensity, by mixing it with a warm or cold colour, or a bit of both?

9. Is the nature of white affected by the colours next to it? Do you find that white takes on some of a complementary of a colour next to it?

10. Here is a list of things to look at for a critical self appraisal. This is rather important for somebody working alone. If you are in classes you have the tutor, some artists, alas, become so dependent on the external appraisal that they cannot work out of art schools. You should always be criticising: tonality, the balance of tones, tones as recession and nearness. Always be looking at 'dessin', the place where drawing intersects with design. Then colour.

11. There is a strange thing about colour. Two persons may work from exactly the same subject, one paints in a muted scheme and the other brilliantly, yet a third person might be indifferent to colour, only painting the sort of tones that might come out in a black and white photo. This is something to be glad about. It does not matter if your colours are not entirely the mirror of nature as long as within the picture space they have a consistency of their own.

12. We have been getting to know a large variety of colours and this could lead you into using all of them or to limiting your palette. Many an excellent painter works with a limited palette.

13. Don't forget that a later chapter gives you complicated techniques that you can be starting to use now. But don't imagine that complication for its own sake will make a good painting. Indeed, look at your painting and ask . . .

14. What can I simplify?

15. Is there any part of the picture that by rubbing over gently with a palette knife could become better for being vague rather than defined? (See Fig. 43.) There are times in an oil painting when passages can be left not so much unpainted but painted ambiguously. The master of this in landscape is of course Turner, what may seem a mere smudge, a hint of a glaze, in context evokes a whole mood.

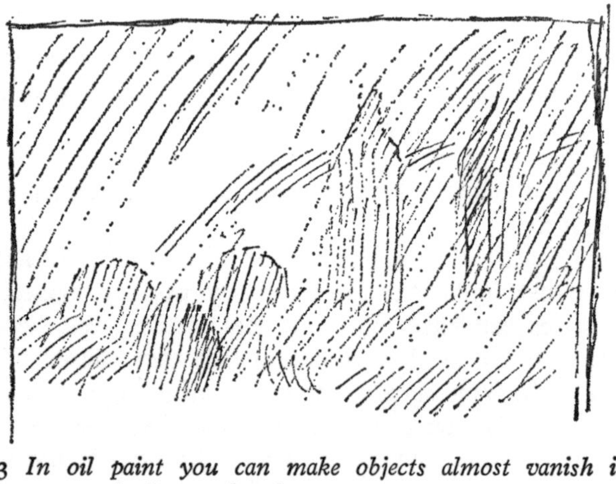

FIG. 43 *In oil paint you can make objects almost vanish into the background and yet appear to emerge.*

16. Even in a formally arranged still life, which appears to leave nothing to chance, you should, when the picture demands it, change what you please, the colour of some fruit or a background.

17. Providing that you are interested in your subject, and equally important, the surface of the picture still invites the touch of your brush, then go on as long as you like.

18. Pace of work. This is like the natural scale at which you work. There are no rules. Some people work fast and others slowly. But it is a good thing, if you fall into one or other category, to try to reverse the process every so often. Slow workers don't tell yourself this is care, it may not be.

19. Care. This does not mean adding irrelevant detail.

20. We as oil painters always come back to the problem of detail. To some this is something one adds on, like veins in a leaf, or the stalk of the apple, the glimmer of light on the glass. Some painters paint like this without compromising the unity of the picture. But this is why in an earlier passage I recommended always exchanging bigger brushes for smaller ones all during the course of the painting. You should try putting in with a small brush, very early on in the course of the painting, something that looks like a detail. It may prove to be a vital element of the whole composition (see Fig. 42(c)).

21. Do the details of light, which are discussed more at length in another chapter, or any intensive copying of detail make a painting photographic? Nothing makes anything photographic except cameras and photosensitive paper. The photographer selects from external phenomena consciously and unconsciously like the painter, but their arts in no way compete.

22. To return to the classical pattern of the still life. The original idea of massing forms to one side to balance the rest as we have done, was originally Titian's invention and was gradually adopted by Rubens and his followers to be the pattern for landscape composition. It was then further developed by Claude Lorraine to have dark masses on both sides of a picture to effect a distance.

23. Many beginners to painting believe there may be some runic alchemic secrets to mixing colour. There may have been in days gone by, but looking for obscure secrets never taught anyone to paint. The rules for mixing are really very few. The best

one is, *don't*. Don't mix for the sake of it. Use a plain colour unmixed whenever you can, but this doesn't happen very often. But still try to use unmixed colours. The reason being that the more you mix colours the less white light is reflected back from the white ground. The more you mix, the more light you are stopping out and the more muddy and discouraging your work becomes. If you have to mix colours do so by the simplest means. Keep your palette clean as this will prevent colours getting turgid and muddy. In a strange, enigmatic quotation from Ingres he says, 'Gentlemen put white in shadows.' I've always interpreted it as against his great rival Delacroix who never did. It is true too that Ingres glazed his colours, so mixing whites in his shadows may not have been so dangerous. But, to put a dab of white indiscriminately the whole time you paint is to end up with a very heavy muddy-looking painting. So think before you mix but especially before you mix with white.

Formal composition or no, or apparently informal, you are always reduced in painting to the four edges of the picture space, which govern all. This confining space you can extend, recede, cover, flatten, but never go beyond.

The masters of the formal composition have been cited enough times in the text but here they are, and please try and see some sort of original, it is worth more than hundreds of colour reproductions.

Raphael, 1483–1520, Umbrain-Roman.
Titian, 1487–1576, Venetian.
Poussin, 1594–1665, Franco-Roman.
Cézanne, 1839–1906, French.
Wash brushes – clean palette!

CHAPTER 7

The Still Life Around You

You are surrounded by the still life. Look, use your eyes, there they are, around you. Rows of cups in kitchens, a jug and fruit on a plate. There are pot plants on the window-sill; there are flowers, charming as they are, on the table before you have arranged them. Perhaps there is a table standing on a beautifully patterned rug or children's brightly coloured toys on cheerful lino. Kitchen chairs, saucepans in a row (see Fig. 44). You do not have to move far, there it all is, a world before you suddenly revealed. Your familiar possessions acquire a new dimension; stripes on a mug suddenly stimulate you to paint; a universe within a grain of sand, indeed. An old geranium in an earthenware pot or a can becomes marvellously beautiful. On this subject, I was forcibly aware of it in Serbia, where the most ordinary cottage, whatever else it did not have, had a geranium in a can on the window sill. The preceding may sound banal, but good works of art are near the commonplace, for these are things to which we will always respond at some level or other. The people to pity are not those who respond to the ordinary, but those who do not; like those highly refined intelligences who can write cleverly or criticise everything, but who never touch upon the true centres of experience. But to return to your world, your kitchen or sitting room, window-sills, to looking. Painting of the great arts is, in the classical definitions, not only active but also contemplative. You should be able to keep a balance between the active and contemplative, and it is time to be active. So you do not have to wait for inspiration. Here it is in front of you, all day. The kind of still life that is around you, you can come across by chance. When you begin to draw or paint, your chance observation has to be confined to the relentless edges of your board, so all elements of chance vanish. If you

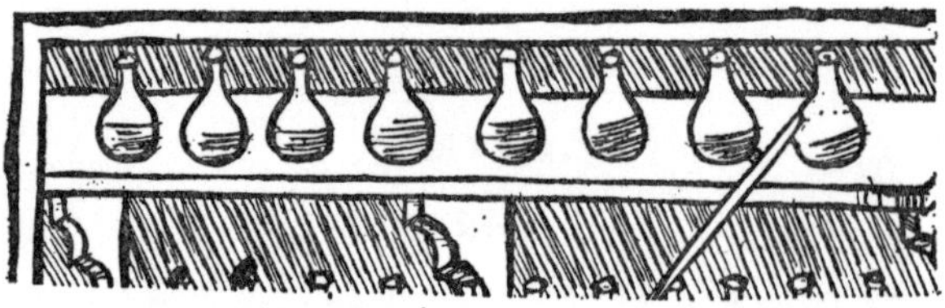

Bottles in a row. from a 15th c woodcut.

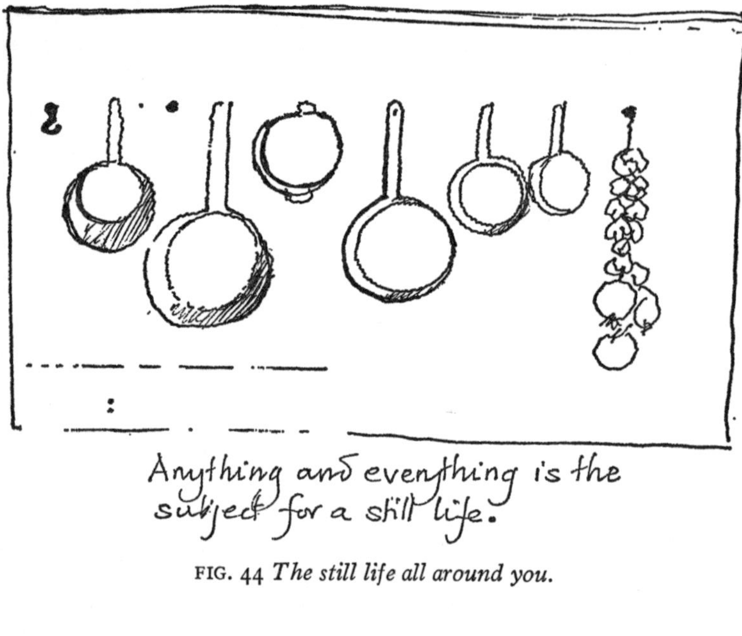

Anything and everything is the subject for a still life.

FIG. 44 *The still life all around you.*

are worrying that this will kill the spontaneity, think of Bonnard's beautiful paintings. There is a painting of a table top in the Tate Gallery, London; it is marvellously evocative of a long, late breakfast that extends into lunch, of an age of leisure and abundance now gone for ever. To look at Bonnard's painting it looks 'dashed off'. But we happen to know that Bonnard took a very long time over his paintings. Only your boredom can kill spontaneity. If you are enjoying painting then every brush mark will be a new and exciting experience. So here you are by a window-sill, or looking at a table with the oddments of cooking or a nice meal. How can this find its way to being a painting?

How to begin. If you are feeling really confident skip this bit and go on to the painting part of the chapter directly. To make things easier, what about using the two pieces of cardboard suggested in Chapter 3, page 60. You can move these around to capture a view that pleases you; in any shape of rectangle.

To sketch before you paint. Start sketching what you saw through the cardboard view-finder. This will help make a composition. As important, it will help you make into shapes and tones what previously had been word. For a beginner it is easy to look at a chance object, say a flower or a newspaper, and then in your mind string a whole trail of words and associations with what you see. In literature this sort of association is very valuable, but very distracting and totally non-communicable if you are drawing and painting. So repress the agreeable and pleasing sensation of making some sort of story of what you see. But what are you seeing? Let us try and answer that. Drawing will help clarify the issue.

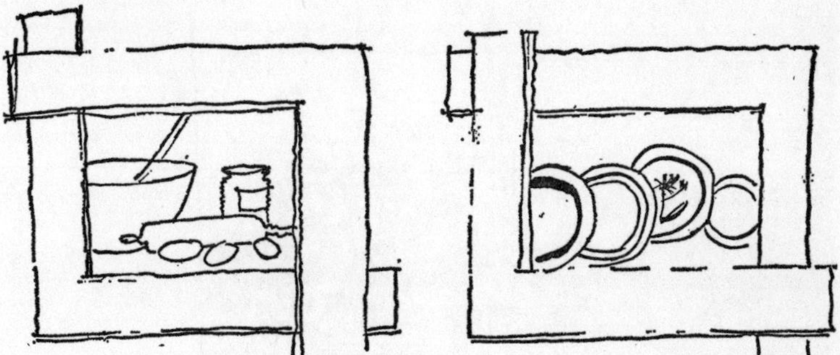

FIG. 45 *With your two L-shaped pieces of cardboard look for patterns and tones everywhere. What shapes to motifs leave out? Don't forget the shape of the board makes a difference too.*

1. *First* draw an outline drawing – was it purely shape for shape? Or pure composition? Yes? No? Whatever you saw the basic composition and drawing are important as all else will follow once these are right. What object attracted you in the first place? How much should you leave out? Can you experiment to advantage with unusual shapes of composition? (Fig. 45.) This can be

a helpful course to pursue, and may show up a bit more about what you are seeing. It is a two-way thing; as you see you draw, and as you draw you see.

2. An unusual shaped composition can give the element of humour. Remember in Chapter 4 on basic design, how the shape of a canvas can effect mood. One that is rather out of the ordinary can quite change your way of seeing.

3. Now do a drawing with tones. Perhaps you will discover it was no particular object that attracted you, but the effect of light. Possibly light coming through a window and falling on to objects, or light shining through flowers. You will still need a basic outline drawing; but now in areas of tone try to show where the light is coming from in relation to where you are sitting. What is the source of the light? See how much it alters the effect of tones if you are looking into the light (see Fig. 46). To make a good picture the tones should be balanced pleasingly.

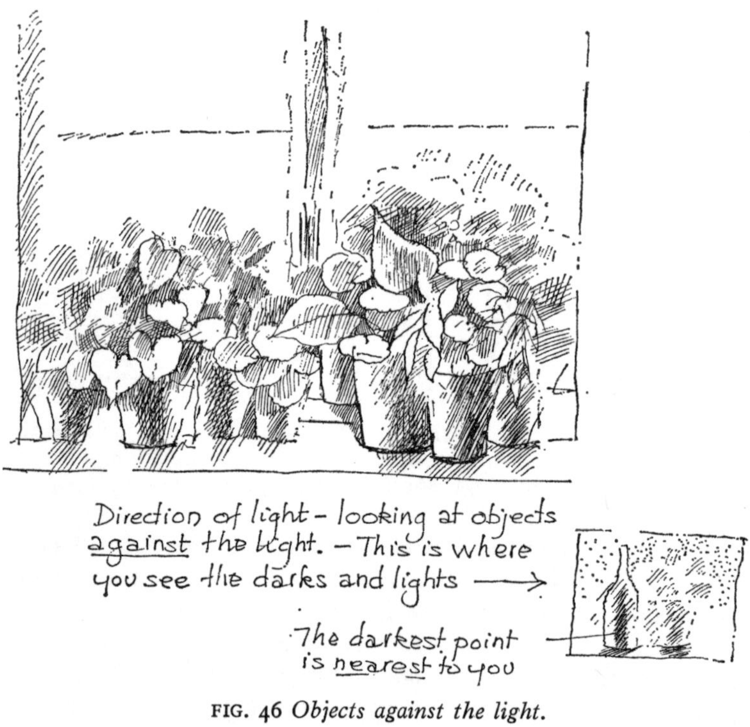

FIG. 46 *Objects against the light.*

To paint. As well as the size and shape of the board there is the question of scale. Until now we have thought more or less in terms of painting in large areas. Perhaps the idea of seeing a charming sight almost by accident might, in its intimacy, lead you to want to paint an intimate picture. Whatever the scale, the difference between this and a formally set-out still life is that of intimacy, a formal still life keeps its distance, as it were.

How to paint the intimate. Of course, your boards have to be smaller. Intimate size is 25 x 20 cm, and lesser dimensions still are miniature. But think of it, if you are somebody who can only snatch moments in which to paint, on this scale you could have the body of a painting in no time. Even if you customarily paint large pictures, it may be the smaller ones that you sell. People often buy small pictures because larger ones might be too large or expensive. If the idea of a small picture appeals to you, you should have plenty of supports prepared because you will probably find you will do lots of paintings. After a time you, who may only have the odd moment to paint, will find that you have a whole collection of little pictures recording for ever marvellous moments of intense experience.

Painting on a small scale means that every brush stroke has far greater significance, and each one is very obvious. Because you paint small there is no need to feel that brush strokes necessarily have to be tiny. Vuillard, master of the intimate painting, used a very broad technique. So on a small scale you can enclose a small world of vision. On an intimate scale you can paint small motifs that would not have very much meaning on a larger scale. This is particularly true of the object one might see by chance. You see something, you would like to catch it but not get seriously involved. Well, you can do this on a very small scale. A little picture of a brief moment of something that pleases you is better than not having any sort of painting at all. Or if you are working on some large and complex picture, it is nice to turn away and dash something off, quickly and carefree. Sometimes a little picture gains from the work you have done on the big one, and the other way about. Do not forget that a small scale picture is no excuse for tinkering and fussiness. The fact that you can always do another little picture if one goes wrong, means that this should be an exercise in breadth. But alternatively, it could be that you may be the sort of painter who, by nature, works small and intimately, delighting in the tiny brush stroke applied with the utmost care. In this case you should always use sable brushes and a very well primed board. For very fine work, board is slightly better than canvas. Even if you are working on a fine scale this does not mean that you are fussy; your brush strokes, however tiny, should be clear and your colour clean. However small your board the principle of beginning with thin paint and working up to thick should still apply. Remember that sable brushes seldom leave much evidence of the brush stroke, and you can get a very smooth enamel-like surface. Many painters working on a very small scale with sable brushes use a technique of putting the paint on in little dots.

Whether you use a broad or minute approach, or something between the two, one of the characteristics of pictures on a small scale is that you can paint things that on a large scale would lose their meaning. If shape of a canvas carries emotional impact so does scale. Right at the other extreme to intimate paintings are the huge paintings of the American abstract expressionists. The great scale of these paintings makes their impact. Another example of scale and meaning is cards with samples of decorators' paints. A postage-stamp size of colour looks quite different when it is painted on a large wall. So to return to the point of a subject losing its meaning on a large scale. There may be the chance sight that is well worth painting in a little picture and yet would look foolish or be a waste of time in a large one. For example, I once painted a pair of jugs, both had jolly spots on them. A small painting had a certain charm, but a large one of the same subject looked silly. The disadvantage of a small picture painted broadly is that it is also easy to give way to bits of carelessness in drawing that would be impossible in a large picture. It is as well therefore, if you like painting small pictures, always to paint a few large pictures that are properly finished from several careful preparatory drawings. Perhaps before you feel you can safely paint intimate paintings, drawings in a little sketch book are a good idea. Like a most personal diary that is written, here is a personal diary that is drawn. The chapter on basic design dealt extensively with shapes within shapes. Now you have to apply this. One of the dangers of reading a book of this kind and attending art schools is keeping lessons separate. This separation is to define the main issues, but all of them relate to one another. So in practical experience, with your sketch book and drawing book, look for *designs around you.* Firstly in flat areas of tone. We mentioned stripy mugs, or dotty jugs (Fig. 47). Fix on some single object. Half shut your eyes, there it is, a tone, a shape. Now draw the tonal shape. Now draw the area round it. Not difficult? Try more objects than one. A couple of cups against bright

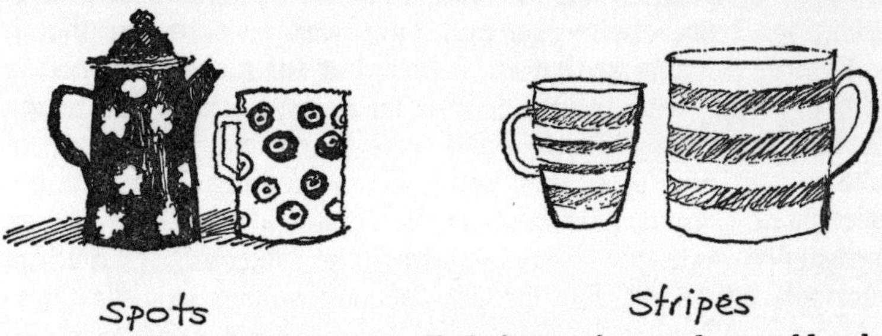

FIG. 47 *Suitable subjects for small, intimate pictures, but could only lose on a large scale.*

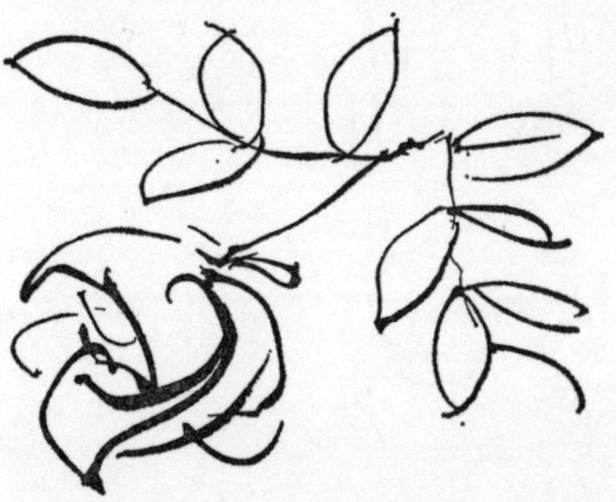

FIG. 48 *A flower left after you have arranged the others – another suitable subject for an intimate painting.*

tiles. Half shut your eyes again, and there you have the tones. There are carefully arranged flowers in one room, and in another room one you did not use lying casually (Fig. 48). It is as much a subject for intimate painting. Of course, in your drawing you can distort proportions just for fun. But I believe one of the delights of intimate painting is grasping the moment of authenticity. Authenticity in this case meaning acuteness of rendering shape for shape, proportion, tone for tone. You must do what you please and if you disagree with this or anything else in the whole book, apart from cleaning up, go ahead your own way. So proportion. You know how to measure. Simple is it not? Otherwise you take a 'norm' of proportion. Decide that one particular *thing* you are looking at is to be a norm, the length of a vertical upright chair-back, or width of a bread-board. Then with this as the norm decide how big or small everything else is in relation to it. With practice, this kind of assessment of a visual problem becomes purely automatic.

The eccentric viewpoint. This is also something that is agreeable in a small sketch, but can often look pointless in a large painting. I say often – you may have seen or done one that is different. A painting that is all floor but for a chair and bed in the top end seems rather foolish on a large scale. The reason is that we usually chance upon these views and in enlargement the greater area of deliberation spoils something. The eccentric viewpoint then can be from an unusually low eye-level, or an unusually high one (see Fig. 49). Or something glanced at through something, like through balcony railings to a view out-

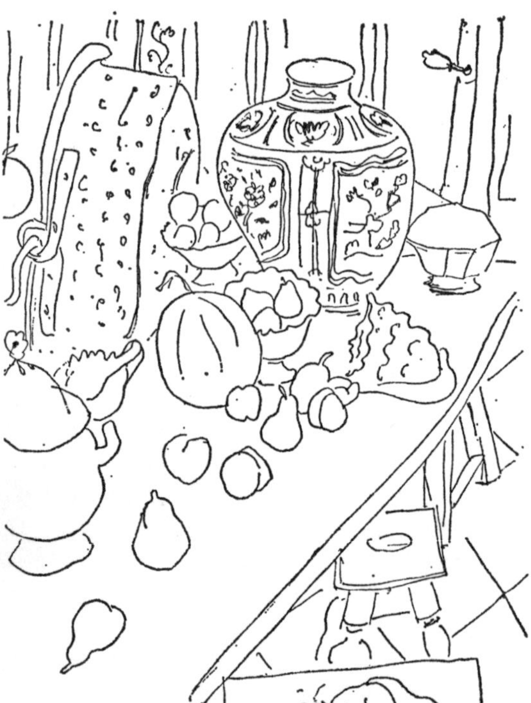

FIG. 49 *The unexpected viewpoint, by Matisse. Copyright SPADEM.*

side. Perhaps the chance grouping of garden tools seen through a half-open door. It is all around you. Use your eyes.

Light. No, not easy. Yet as mentioned on page 112 what *can* catch our eye is a glimmer of light on an object, sun shining through the pot plants. To take the latter. You are looking into the light. If you do not let it become a dangerous habit of, on a larger scale, leaving tracks of canvas unfinished, you can borrow a technique from the water colourists. Leave the white areas of the board for the light and paint the rest in very thin paint. Another way of rendering light is working on tinted boards.

Tinted boards. Many a painter, after first having primed boards white, has afterwards added a final coat of tinted priming. More about this on page 140. What in effect this does is to give you the ready-made middle tone. All you then need do is draw the shapes in the colours of the highlights and darks (Fig. 50). A middle tone saves time if you are in a hurry. Sometimes, even the very look of being unfinished gives the picture its charm.

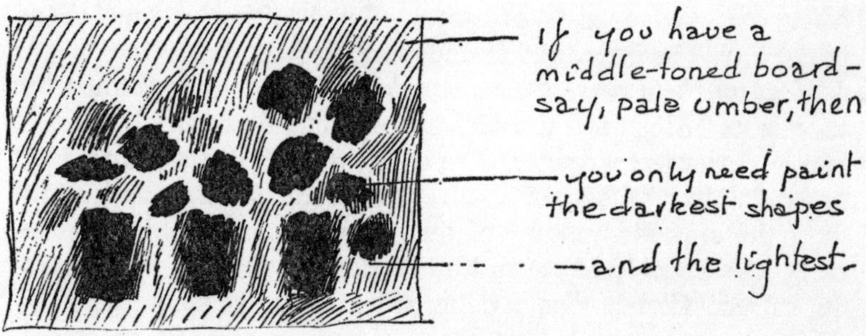

FIG. 50 *Using a middle-toned board.*

But what is unfinished? On the intimate scale, when your picture has summed up the exact atmosphere without recording too much, or when the effect is pleasing. Providing you keep a balance between this and large-scale finished work, you can always profitably leave some paintings unfinished. What is left and suggested, the artist and the beholder finish in their imagination, herein lies the danger and the fascination to the artist.

From smaller to larger. A little painting may not have explored the full possibilities of your subject. So to enlarge.

Bonnard who was, in his early years, classified as an intimist, ended up by painting fairly large intimate pictures, about 90 x 150 cm or so. The subjects he chose were intimate. Bonnard is the most marvellous teacher for the painter for pleasure. His paintings grew from his surroundings. Like his friend and contemporary, Vuillard, he never strayed from home; he was untouched by the heroic and grand. Your paintings too, can grow from your surroundings. A large painting can grow from a sketch and still be intimate. With Bonnard, the intimacy is evolved from his surroundings and the surface of the board, his eye and his hand. So, whenever you feel that a small sketch is not adequate to express the full possibilities of a subject, transpose it to a larger board. Do not forget the points made earlier, that change of scale can totally affect the emotional impact of subject matter and the characters of colours. Remember too, that if you paint some chance object, it can tell you more about a place then a grandiose town- or sea-scape. I mentioned Serbia before. Once, after a vain struggle with a painting of a vast plain and mountains, on visiting a little house I painted the coffee pot and a glass of water offered with the usual Slav hospitality. The little still life said more.

How much to paint from the subject. This is only learned by experience. Most art schools, at any rate those in the U.K., have a curious programme. The students work directly from life, never painting without the subject in front of them, and go to the quite opposite extreme of total abstraction. Indeed, in some cases it is considered untruthful to do any painting away from the subject. Clearly that is rather silly. There are many excellent painters who can only sort out a picture in some of its stages by painting away from the subject. Providing the end result is consistent and good, this is the only truth that matters. We know that Bonnard had to work long and intensely away from the subject. Sadly, the discipline of *working from drawings* has even gone out of art-school training. You are very restricted if you cannot work from drawings, though it is less important in the still life than in history pictures and the portrait. The chapters on drawing have tried to give the basic elements. We must not at any time, any of us, forget the words 'disegno' and 'dessin' which, in the Latin cultures, rightly refuse to distinguish between drawing and design. But, there comes a point where it is difficult for anyone to tell the artist the type of information he will need from a drawing to do a successful painting. I happen to believe that an accurate outline gives nearly all. You may not agree. Simply, the only way to learn to do drawings to paint from is to start to paint as soon as you can from a drawing, say of a chance view in the kitchen. You will find out soon enough what the drawing is not telling you, I mean *you,* no one else. Many painters, Rembrandt was one, find drawing in pen and ink more nearly relates to painting than a harder, less flexible medium. But do *not* let current art-school teaching put you off this most essential branch of learning how to paint.

Painting from photographs. In other books, in an attempt to meet the tastes of a reader, I did not, at least, discourage this. Now for a committed opinion. *DON'T.* A stint of marking art examination papers showed a most depressing dependence on photographs. Be inspired by photographs or anything else. But do not paint from photographs, in the end it will stop you looking for yourself. Even if you have taken the photograph yourself it is not a good idea but, presumably, if you insist I cannot stop you.

Scale of paintings. It may be that you are unable to work very big or very small. This is a question of eye-sight and you can only learn by trying. Some painters can only work very small, even miniature; miniature still lifes have enormous appeal. In the list below the tiny intimate still life appears largely to be a phenomenon of the twentieth century. Does it represent a proper and understandable reaction on the part of the creative artist to the impersonal age we live in?

Wash brushes and clean palette!

Intimate painters. Look especially at Bonnard or Vuillard. If you live in the U.K., the small south gallery at The Royal Academy of Arts has enchanting intimate still lifes. Look out particularly for Margaret Green, Bernard Dunstan, R.A. and Eliot Hodgkin.

CHAPTER 8

Studies Around the Still Life

If you have read the other books in the series, there is always a chapter on the still life, however apparently remote from the main subject of the book. The still life is treated as an aspect of painting where you can always return to basic reality. You may feel that you are a portrait painter, but if you have not got a portrait to paint there is nothing like painting an apple to remind you of simple rounded forms. In Chapter I that somewhat unfashionable of subjects, the full-scale epic figure composition, was described as the highest form of art. A less ambitious study in composition is the complex still life. So in this chapter we work outward from the still life. Throughout the book we have been referring to the seventeenth-century Dutch artists, and this leads into an aspect of developing the still life.

From still life to the interior. The seventeeth-century Dutchman conserved and husbanded the land like a craftsman. He was a maker of lenses and mirrors. A mirror recreates and extends the world and the dolls' houses and peep-show boxes of seventeenth-century Holland recreated the world in miniature. The Dutch interior painting does exactly the same, though paintings of interiors were not new in the low countries. We are familiar with interiors in annunciations of fifteenth-century Flemish paintings, or in a painting like J. Van Eyck's *The Chancellor Rollin Adoring Our Lady.* In the fifteenth century all representation of reality contained the deepest symbolism; three windows were the Trinity; flowers were always in the language of symbols. The Flemings may have thought that a recreation of reality in somebody praying to Our Lady was a reminder to Our Lady herself, so powerful in those days was the symbolic image. The interiors of the seventeenth century were direct descendants of these paintings. Depth and reality were recreated in oil paint, and among the many differences was that the seventeenth-century paintings were usually secular. Symbolism survived fitfully, sometimes in the Christian doctrinal sense, sometimes more related to heraldry and to others on a personal level. By 'personal' I mean the objects that are associated with one person. To return to still life as part of an interior; it is not only something we can associate with seventeenth-century Holland but also with the School of Paris *c.* 1890–1930. In particular

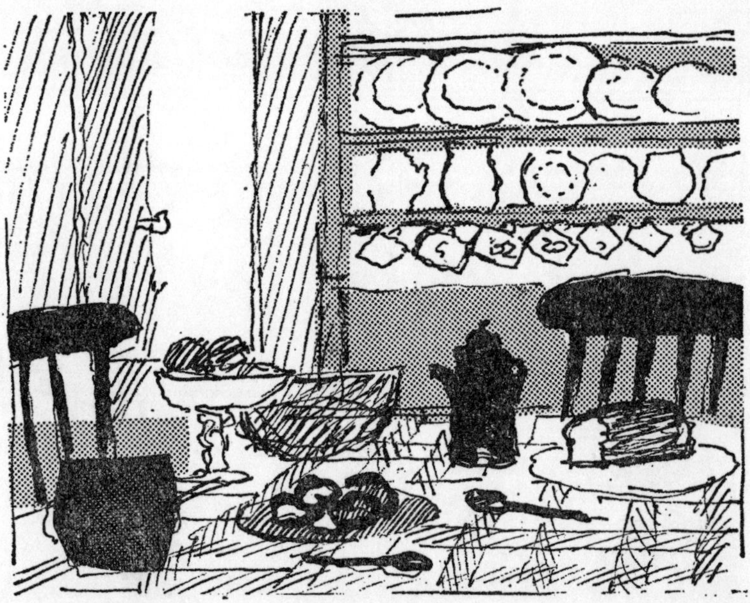

FIG. 51 *How a still life can become an interior.*

Bonnard and Matisse, whose tables laden with delicious food extended into rooms and gardens. While looking at the old Dutch paintings and the modern French painters to inspire your work, you should begin painting yourself. A lot of what we will be considering intersects with Chapters 6 and 7 but this always happens. It is not difficult to see how a still life becomes an interior (see Fig. 51).

From still life to the exterior. Often you can find a ready-made picture framed by a window and the objects on the window-sill, a case of a still life becoming a townscape or landscape. This sort of subject could be treated as shapes of colour-tones. In the way that the cubists or Matisse would have taken easily recognised motifs and transposed them into a pattern. This is not to suggest that you mimic these or any other painters; they are only to start you off. It is a very good starting point to make you want to paint, not an imitation, but one of your own. The drawings in Fig. 52 give you an idea of how to think

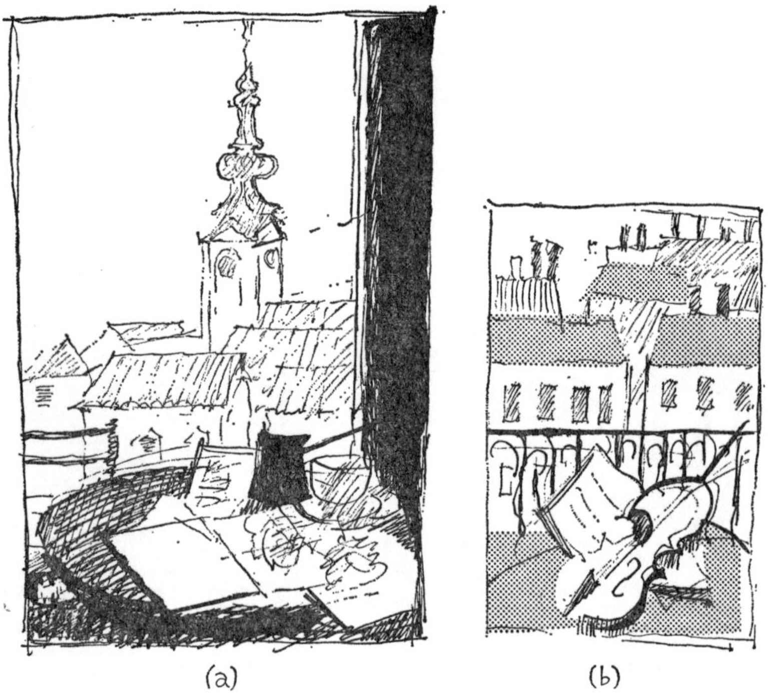

FIG. 52 *From still life to exterior.* (a) *The near-to objects will be larger and more sharply contrasted in tone. The window makes the frame. Linear perspective in the distance will be less pronounced.* (b) *You could treat the problem as one of abstract shapes, dispensing with conventional perspective.*

of designing a painting of this kind. This does not exclude, and indeed is part of, treating the subject directly from the visual sensation. In effect, looking and translating what you see in terms of canvas and paint.

Painting directly from the object seen. Preliminary sketches are always useful. Some may be very similar to the illustrations 52(a) and (b). Where there is a ready-made frame of a window, etc., the problem of composition is not difficult. To contain a distance, to effect greater depth by a dark framing foreground, is an artifice invented by Claude (1600–82). In this case, he, and his many followers, surrounded the distance by a frame of trees, rocks, architecture. But you will be using the framework of the window.

Now to paint. Up till now the still lifes we have been painting from direct observation have been painted with the light falling on them. We are now looking from dark into light, which will affect tone and colour quite differently. Firstly, shadows will fall in different places. You should look to see if the shadows are a darker version of the colours in the light, or contain colours in their own right. I mean look, for while the impressionists taught us to look for colours in shadows, we should not take their vision as correct if it contradicts what we see. From my experience I notice a complete ambivalence in painting shadows directly from the object seen. There are darks, but the darks contain colour, there are colours but they are sometimes the opposite of those in the light and sometimes the same. This is very conspicuous when you are looking from the dark into the light. Much of this may seem paradoxical; as creativity is often about contradictions, and painting is about resolving them. As I write, I look on to the white paper. It is duller in tone than a bright cloud seen from the window, an effect that happens quite often; it defies the maxim that the nearer to your eye an object is the sharper the tonal contrast. So how would you make a distant, bright object look further away than a near-to one that is subdued? There are two answers. One is by scale, that near-to objects are larger. An obvious instance, a vase that you know is smaller than a tree will look larger as it is nearer to you. And the other is that if a picture works by breaking the rules, then the picture works as an autonomous work of art, and so leave it as it is. Interiors extending into views are often from an artist's own studio; they have a sort of autobiographical intimacy that is part of their charm and appeal.

From still life to landscape. It is a good enough achievement to paint a view. Many attractive views have been painted in the twentieth century, but not many landscapes have. A view is not a landscape. A landscape, as apart from a view, is a panorama of earth and water and air. It reflects man's interpretation of nature and the elements. This may not have much in common with man in the late twentieth century. The great ages of landscape painting were done in times when people generally believed in an ordered universe. When Cézanne wrote about the landscape that 'Pater Omnipotentem' spreads before us, he used the language of an ordered, authoritative, humanistic tradition – Latin. The established artists of the twentieth century may not paint landscape, or anything else from the external world. People who paint because they want to in their own time, still paint landscapes. This may be you, preserving in your own way a major art that has been neglected by others. So to return to life and landscape.

You may have seen in galleries and in reproductions still lifes arranged against a background of actual landscape. One I can think of is by Delacroix and the other by Renoir. The first is of gamebirds against an autumn background; the other is pretty fruit where the soft, transparent oil paint hints at a hot summer's day. The main idea is the portrait (to put it that way) of the objects. The landscape can give extension and mood. The landscape is usually a colour to evoke a mood, and both pictures described have seasonal backgrounds. There are certain colours we associate with the seasons and these could set the whole mood of a still life (see Fig. 53). A colour scheme can give unity even if a composition cannot. Another example where a still life by a quite unknown artist can take one's fancy. I remember seeing in a very old copy of *Studio* a picture of a sea still life. Grey and pink shells, and fish set against a grey sea. No great work of art but one was glad it was painted. Perhaps one day somebody will feel like that about one of your paintings. In a painting of this kind a degree of composition is important. That is to say, how much can you allow the landscape to take up the picture space? The answer is any amount you like providing you like the balance and look of the picture. As long as the painting looks right you only have to suggest the atmosphere of the landscape. This, as you may have worked out for yourself, is done by glazes of very soft, gentle paint and by scumbling too. There is no rule but the pictures of still life in landscape most usually have the background in duller, lighter

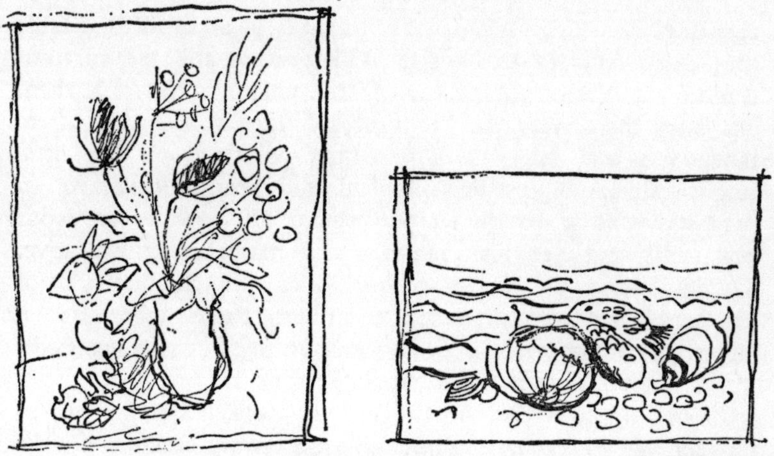

FIG. 53 *Associative subjects can be painted in colour schemes you associate with them, e.g. the still life of dried winter flowers, or of marine objects.*

tones to give the effect of distance. It is in softness and suggestion that oil paint wins time and again over acrylic paints. Atmosphere and light are the expressions on the body of landscape. The structure of the body of landscape is geology. If you are a serious landscape painter you should learn a little geology. But there is not space here to go into it. Instead, where still life intersects with the structure of landscape is in the still lifes of Cézanne. If the idea appeals, you can study structure through the folds of drapery (see Fig. 54). Obviously, the end result will not be a landscape painting, but you will be training your eye and hand to interpret structure and mass.

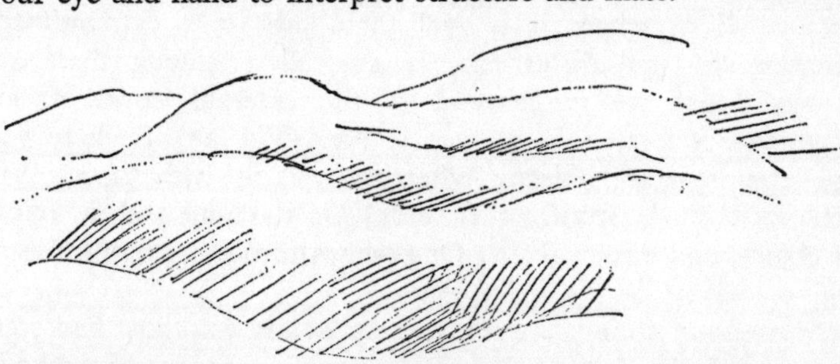

FIG. 54 *While drawing the folds of drapery think of the undulations of landscape.*

From still life to interior. The introduction described an interesting, if not very good, early example of a still life – a table that extended into an interior. This sort of still life survived throughout seventeenth-century Dutch painting. Not only then, but later there were the beautiful still lifes of Bonnard where tables ran into interiors. The Dutch paintings are like little bright mirrors, everything clarified and beautifully drawn in perspective. Bonnard ignores perspective. His space is not depth but area; and yet his paintings are marvellously evocative. Coming back to the chapter on basic design you can have a lot of fun just looking at the shapes of interiors chairs, tables, doors, and see how they will all go in a picture. As Picasso once said: 'As for the things so much the worse for them'.

From fruit to nudes. An Indian love poem, a London costermonger and Renoir have all compared a downy peach to a girl's backside. Renoir painted pretty fruit and flowers because they reminded him of a girl's skin. But we have to be practical. Renoir was a meticulous painter, always taking care that his palette and brushes were scrupulously clean. You will notice that his colours never go dense and muddy, he never uses many darks in his shadows. Another of his techniques is to paint very transparently in glazes. But do not forget that Renoir's apparent facility came after relentless and serious study in the life class and from the antique.

From the real to beyond the real. One of the longest surviving art movements of the twentieth century is surrealism. It is figurative painting, but not based on analysing the external world or synthesising, idealising or directly representing it. Instead it is based on the sort of thing we are supposed to see in dreams. Even where it is real there are some extraordinary discrepancies and distortions. In surrealist painting there are always things we recognise from the external world of our experience yet put in a strange context (Fig. 55). So here you are, your still life objects. What can you do with them? Will you put them in strange surrounds? Or start out with a couple of objects and distort them? Or perhaps turn them into a dream with associated images and objects?

Surrealist paintings are private images and you must find your own way. If you believe there is a common language of symbolic dream objects you could make up a still life of these. The dream

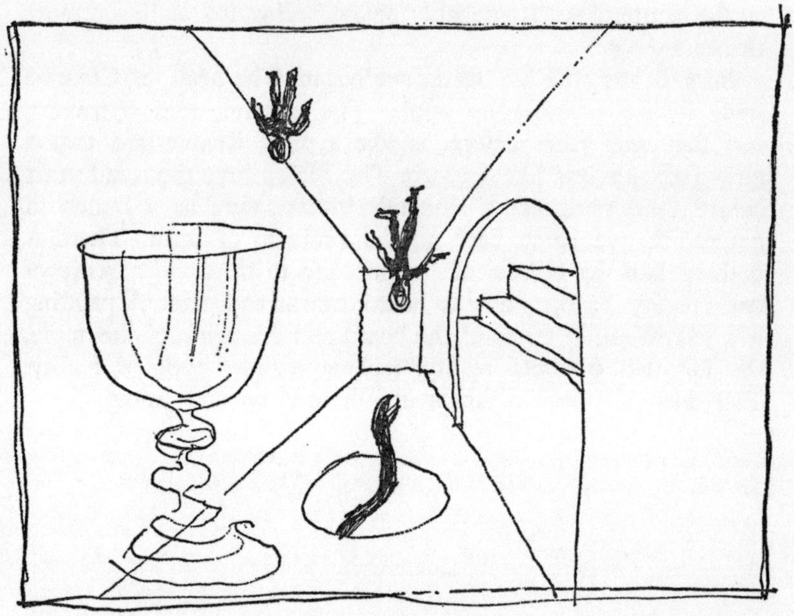

FIG. 55 *Surrealism – by distorting or putting objects from the real world in strange contexts you can create a self-contained world of fantasy.*

work can be infinitely large or infinitely small. In a surrealist painting you can create a universe of your own on its own terms. The infinitely small. Perhaps this is an extension of plant drawing but many a contemporary artist has painted the world of the microscope. The structure of cells, crystals, molecules, snowflakes, it is a list that could go on indefintely. It works the other way about, that many modern paintings remind us of this world too. I think in particular of Mark Tobey, an American painter, whose purely abstract paintings could remind you of the world opened up by electronic microscopy. These paintings, directly and indirectly inspired by the microscope, are pleasing, but that is about all. If put to it I would say that the province of the painter is what can be seen with the natural eye in normal scale, but you must try anything you please. Reading a book of how it's done it is usual to get something quite different out of it than ever the author thought of or probably intended, but as long as you get something, and those around you too. Like taking a child to the pantomime, it probably enjoys seeing the audience more than the show.

Back to the still life, where we began. The head, as Cézanne said, is like painting an apple. The column, said Vitruvius, two thousand years before, is like a man; Renoir said that a girl's backside was like a peach. The Bible, three thousand years before that, said that a woman's breasts were as a bunch of grapes. So we come back to the problem of form. There is nothing like the objects of the still life to tie us to a sense of basic reality. So back now to board, canvas and paint. A painting is a recreation, in terms of the board and the paint, of the apple, the jug and concrete reality, making another type of reality. This does not mean detachment – there is no such thing.

CHAPTER 9

Drawing and Painting Flowers

Drawing flowers. Flowers are so much part of painting that you may be wondering why there is a separate heading. One very good reason is that it is a very good way of learning to do straightforward accurate drawings which, because of their stringent accuracy, have aesthetic appeal in their own right. Once you can make an accurate flower drawing, you will find no difficulty whatever in intricate drawings for still life objects, and what with solid geometric shapes and now plant drawing you have a very sound basis. In any case many of you may have admired lovely flower prints and now want to do a fine flower drawing in the same way. The flower print has a function. It was made by a botanist, who presented his information relevantly and clearly, so that somebody seeing it who did not know the individual flower, would at least be able to place it in its family of flowers. Botanical illustration is probably as old as writing, and flower patterns existed before that. The purpose has always been useful. Until the middle of the nineteenth century, dyes and medicines came from plants and were produced largely domestically, so households, monasteries, etc., were dependent on these herbals. Before the invention of printing, herbals were in manuscript, and after the invention of printing the illustrations were first in woodcuts and later in metal engravings. You see very fine old woodcuts were the plant is made to fit the basic wood block. The great ages of botanical illustration were the seventeenth, eighteenth and nineteenth centuries. These were the ages which saw the rise of the biological sciences, new botanical gardens and discoveries from abroad of new plants. These fine engravings and drawings are now prized as art works in their own right, and this is understandable. It is equally rewarding to look at them for the purpose that they were done, and to see Thornton and Redoute as fulfilling the highest standards demanded by the botantists' art. What then are these standards? It could be described as clear, unfussy presentation of the main forms of the flower, with all the subsidiary forms subjected to this. A botanical drawing differs from a life or portrait study as you are recording information and not recreating life. Plant drawing can be learned with a fair amount of diligence. If this is all that you ever learn to paint you will not have done too badly. Indeed, you will have done jolly well, giving yourself and others considerable pleasure more cheaply than oil painting. Many Victorian oddments, now sold for huge sums, were decorated with pretty flowers by young ladies at home, and you could do the same making life prettier and more pleasant all round. Learning flower painting was a normal part of young ladies' education, and their impoverished painting masters only survive in fiction!

Equipment. Your first ventures into plant studies should be with modest equipment. A medium grade pencil very well sharpened, and a reasonable quality cartridge paper neither too rough nor too smooth, *no* rubbers.

Dexterity. Plant drawing requires a fair degree of manual dexterity and you could easily look up the exercises on page 39. During the twentieth century there has been a deep revulsion against dexterity. The most popular and influential draughtsmen of our age, Moore, Picasso, Klee, all share a rugged line. Slickness has been confused with dexterity. Slickness is a state of mind, dexterity is the right degree of bodily control.

The main forms. The main forms of a plant are the first things that you should look for. In the illustrations (Fig. 56) are some of the main types of plant growth, as well as some exercises as these may be helpful too. These exercises relate to botanical structure, but for those of you who are going on to oil painting it's worth having a look at the shapes as they are useful for analysing the solid form of the flower.

If you look at an ordinary good text-book of wild flowers you see clear totally comprehensible line drawings, but which could not be called works of art. Yet so little would make them art works. The little that is the all, that lies in the margin of sensibility that divides the competent from the inspired. What you usually see in an ordinary text-book is the plain, quite unvaried

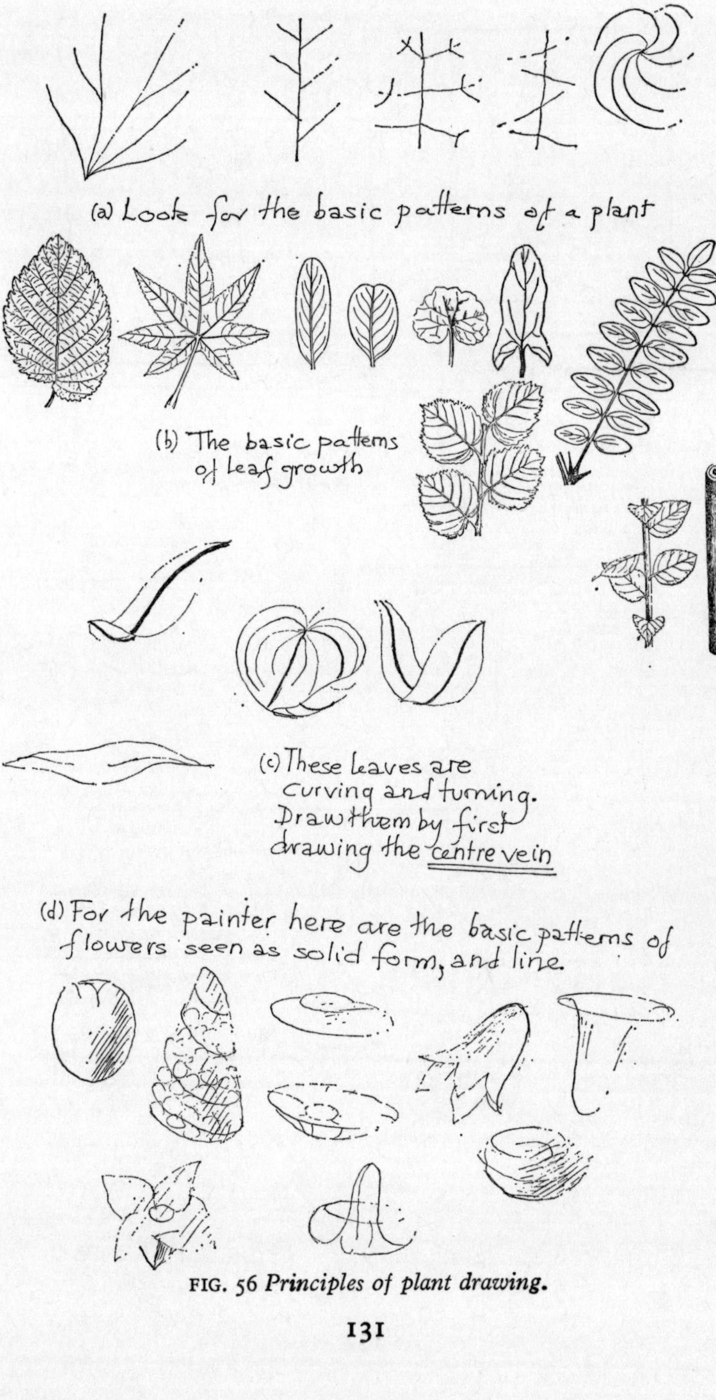

FIG. 56 *Principles of plant drawing.*

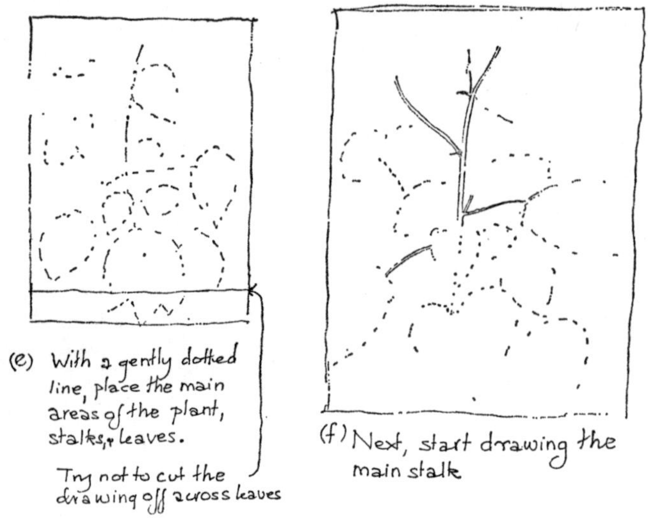
(e) With a gently dotted line, place the main areas of the plant, stalks, + leaves.
Try not to cut the drawing off across leaves
(f) Next, start drawing the main stalk

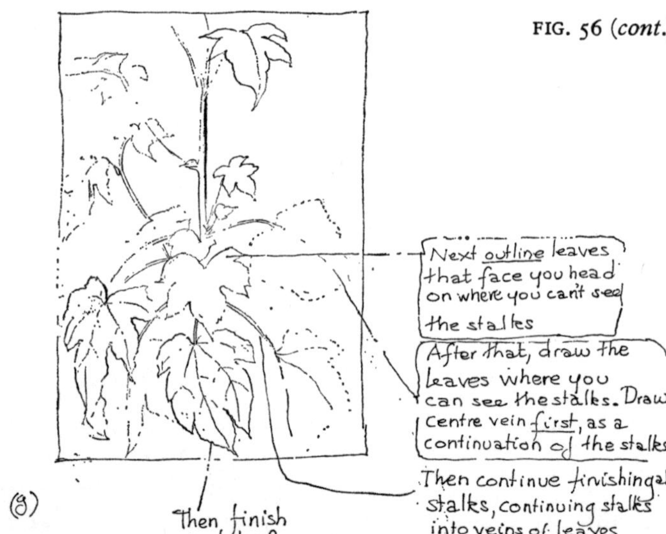
Next outline leaves that face you head on where you can't see the stalks
After that, draw the leaves where you can see the stalks. Draw centre vein first, as a continuation of the stalks
Then continue finishing all stalks, continuing stalks into veins of leaves
(g)
Then finish each leaf.

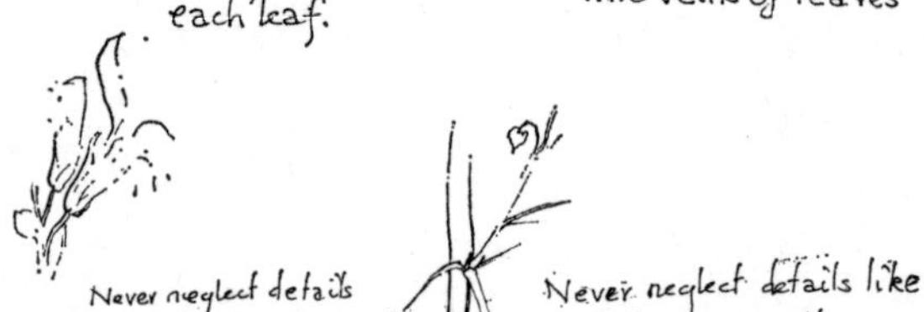
Never neglect details of sepals etc.
Never neglect details like axillary growths

FIG. 56 (*cont.*)

outline. So you should practise the emphasis of line, with variations of thick and thin. A softer pencil, handled with care, has greater tonal variation than a hard one.

To start drawing. You can learn plant drawing by methodical application, so methodically ordered equipment will set you off to a good start. Your paper should be steady, well clipped or pinned on to a board.

The plant. To start with, if you are really a beginner, you had better choose a pot plant, or some ivy, or something that won't die on you before you have finished a reasonable session of work. It is not worth trying to be clever and trying to draw from a complicated viewpoint or some eccentric angle. Choose a straightforward view. Remember that a plant agreeably arranged on the page looks better than one that isn't. A fact that reminds us of basic design, that what you leave out is as important as what you put in! Your drawing should attempt to be life size. One day you may need these drawings to make paintings from. We know that de Gheyn, the Dutch painter, always painted his tulips from drawings because of the prodigious cost of the lovely blooms. A plant drawing that is out of scale looks not wrong but odd, you would not draw a pimpernel the size of a rose.

The illustrations give you the basic instructions for a very reasonable guide as to how to go about plant drawing. When you had a look at perspective this was a guide too. Only your vision as an artist can give these formulas personality and dimension of spirit. There is nothing like learning a scheme to invent one for yourself. The line drawing could stand as it is, and there is no need to fill in with fussy shading, and shading should only be added where it explains forms, not as a disguise for weak drawing. Your first effort at plant drawing may not be going as you wish but you should keep at it even if it is looking forced and laboured. If you really want to do plant drawing and feel it is the thing that will give you pleasure, then do keep at it as you will be astonished at how much easier it gets with practice. You could try to do a plant drawing regularly, even twice a week. At the beginning it is worth forming sound habits. Where the illustration says do not ignore or be careless of this sort of detail it means it. You can be careless if you want to but don't blame me if it gets worse. Later on there's a fair bit for you if you like the idea of splashy flowers or just flowers, but you should do some serious drawings of flowers sometimes. Accurate observation of relevant detail is one of the highest faculties given to creative artists and scientists. So too is classification which, of course, is part of botany and every science. As an artist you may in the end invent your own private system of classifying plants. It may be that after a while you may decide that plant drawing requires a sort of patience, a sort of abnegation of personality that is not for you. With so many aspects of painting or drawing you never know till you have tried. One learns at many levels, and where one thinks that one's studies are least fruitful, one can unconsciously be absorbing much that will one day come back in quite some other way. Your mind was working at a level you knew not. Of course you may find that you have a genuine talent for flower drawing, so that next step is . . .

Colouring plant drawings and be warned, you will mess up some very agreeable pencil drawings before you get the real hang of it. This always happens when you learn something new. It destroys what you knew before and then you reach a dreadful stage where you cannot go back, and going forward is worse, but this is quite usual and then later you find you have even greater skill than before. Like the sort of language you can pick up somehow and chatter away to order from a waiter, and you find you need the grammar to sort out the bill. So back to colour. Not coloured crayons but . . .

Artists' Water Colour. By this I mean fine water colour, where the character of every colour depends on its fineness and transparency. The tiny grains of colour are suspended in the water. Students' Water colours will not do, they are coarsely ground, and when dissolved in water look gritty. Here to start with is a list of basic artists' water colours. Ultramarine, lemon yellow, viridian, raw umber, yellow ochre, cadmium red and quinacridone magenta. This is basic.

Brushes. You never can economise on these. Fine sables only. You will want a couple of medium small and one or two very small.

Paper. The fortunate artists of the great ages of water colour painting had one advantage over us. The only paper available was hand made. Fine water colour painting depends quite as much on fine paper as on fine paint. You will need a smooth surface, hand-made paper to paint a really fine flower study, though for practice you could stick to cartridge. When you are experienced enough to feel you can use fine water colour paper you will be amazed at the difference.

Basic techniques of traditional water colour. By 'traditional' we mean the water colour techniques that were invented by the English water colourists of the nineteenth century. The basic principle is using the white of the paper for absolute white. Instead of mixing colours with white to lighten them, you dilute them with water, the white paper shining through the thin film of paint. This means that while you can darken a pale film of colour you cannot lighten a dark one. You can't improvise, you have to have a clear idea of what you are going to do before you begin. If you do a fair and regular amount of practice in water colour technique then thinking in terms of the technique will become automatic. You have to think in terms of the medium's limitations, not inspite of them.

Water not so obvious I needn't mention it. It is vitally important that you have plenty of clean clear water.

Stretching paper. To paint really craftsmanly water colours you should stretch your paper so that it does not cockle disagreeably as soon as you start painting. To stretch paper it should be placed on a clean drawing board. Sponge the whole surface with swift light strokes using a sponge dipped in water. Do not rub the surface. Turn the paper over and sponge the other side. See that the sponge flattens the paper and presses out all the air bubbles but without rubbing the surface. Pin the edges of the paper to the board with lots and lots of drawing pins, or stick all the edges down with gum strip. The paper can be used to any degree of wetness, though if you are doing clear accurate work you will want to use dry paper.

Some exercises in the techniques of water colour are given in Fig. 57. When you have done these then painting a flower will come easily. When you are faced with the actual flower it is a good idea to paint in, when you begin, the very darkest parts of the flower. This establishes the tonal range of the flower. If you have the very darkest and the very lightest then you can match up the other colour tones more easily.

Mixing water colour. Again the rule is: don't unless you have

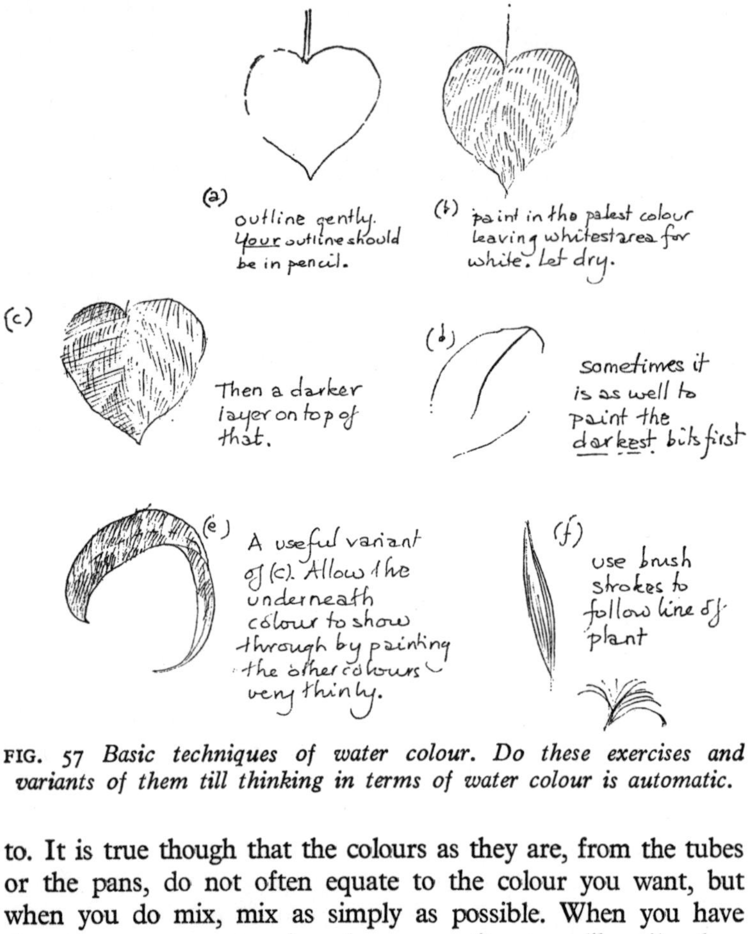

FIG. 57 *Basic techniques of water colour. Do these exercises and variants of them till thinking in terms of water colour is automatic.*

to. It is true though that the colours as they are, from the tubes or the pans, do not often equate to the colour you want, but when you do mix, mix as simply as possible. When you have the colour you want, mix a large quantity as unlike oil colour water colours can be dissolved again with water when they have dried on the palette.

Painting with water colour. If you want the colour to spread on the paper, then paint on to wet paper. If you are doing accurate work, then wait till the paper is thoroughly dry. There are some flower painters who say that as they are not covering the paper with lots of watery paint as they paint the flowers, they do not even stretch the paper. The finest water colours depend on clear decisive thinking. But if you are drawing flowers, or for that matter anything else that requires precision, once you use water colour, it is a very good idea to draw the outline of the flower lightly in pencil first. Use a hard pencil, as the water will dissolve the lead of a soft pencil making the colour dirty. One of the pleasures of water colour is putting the colour on in layers so that the layer below shows through. You get different effects of course depending on whether the under layer of paint has dried or not. If you find you have natural facility with water colour, you could even do the preliminary drawing in brush and paint first. Not that natural facility is that important in water colour, but a genuine *feel* for traditional water colour is. You have to feel as much about the texture of the paper and a sable brush in watery paint as the thing seen. There are many excellent artists who do not have this feel. But there is nothing to be lost by trying the basics of genuine water colour.

Water colour gouache. This is a way of using white for lights in water colour. Water colour gouache is artists' water colour mixed with Chinese white and is perfectly suitable for colouring flower drawings; many an excellent botanical illustration has been coloured in this way. This technique of using Chinese white is not to be confused with poster or design gouache which are much coarser media. The effect, or course, of using the Chinese white in the mixing is to make the colours opaque. Therefore you do not have to be so meticulous about building the colour up from light to dark. The gouache is opaque so you can cover up your mistakes. Gouache is inclined to dry slightly lighter than it looks when it is wet. The rule of never mixing more paints together than you need to applies here as well. Gouache is also not so dependent on the quality of the paper, so you can use it on fine cartridge as well as hand-made water colour paper. You can also paint flower studies on a coloured ground. 'Ingres' and 'Tumba' paper (described on page 36) are admirable for this. A very pale flower or fruit study on a soft darker paper is most attractive. Flower paintings in gouache can be varnished if you like the idea of flowers as decoration for handicrafts.

Another look at flower painting. When you look at flowers, perhaps wild ones in a meadow, or spring blossom against a sky, this may not inspire you to a meticulous study. Your feelings are what are making you an artist, and are therefore very important. Maybe you want to get the spontaneity and happiness that flowers make you feel, and never mind accuracy. So you will want to paint as spontaneously as you feel. So here is quite another approach, not a contradiction to what went before, but one of the polarities we find in ourselves as much as in painting. Light and shadow, white and black, calm and agitated, we have seen premeditation, now spontaneity. You remember about stretching the paper? This time, do not wait for it to dry. With larges brushes mix in plenty of water with the colours of the flowers, they do not have to be strictly accurate, just the colours you feel. Now freely paint the colour in shapes, as you think right, on the paper; suggest the shapes of the colours of the flowers and leaves. You will notice that when painting on wet paper the paint floats and dissolves in the water most engagingly. For best effects you do have to leave the paint be, and not mess it about on the paper once you have painted it on. It might be as well too, not to forget the basic rule that to make water colour really luminous it is best to start with the palest, and build up to the darker. In this sort of painting in no way feel any compulsion to go on once the painting looks right, instead paint another, and another, and more! But can one go on painting more or less intuitively without refreshing oneself with exercises and deliberately planned work. Do so if you want to, but I believe that our inspiration and intuition come from consciously and unconsciously acquired knowledge from regular and disciplined work.

Today, the most popular works of Albrecht Durer, 1471–1526, are his drawings: his praying hands, his hare and of course his plant drawings. Like Leonardo da Vinci, every aspect of the external world interested him and like Leonardo he wrote a treatise on proportion. His major works were his etchings and engravings, which are the portraits of his age too, in their air of religion, trouble, humanism and enquiry. Durer has compared the artist to the life of a plant, that it puts down roots, takes grafts and then has flowers after its kind. And that is exactly what we as artists are like. We need manure as much as the blooms and the pruning knife. The extension of plants goes to trees. But this is the province of landscapes.

CHAPTER 10

More About Painting Flowers

This chapter is concerned primarily with two special cases of flower painting, directly extended from the preceding chapter. The first section deals with the flower paintings in the Dutch style. We are all familiar with the beautiful seventeenth-century Dutch flower paintings, and deplorably familiar with cheap, bad twentieth-century imitations sold in department stores. One thing is clear. The seventeenth-century paintings are not better just because they are old but because, of course, they are better observed and painted. The sale of cheap modern paintings cannot entirely be dismissed, it is a tribute to the original, demonstrating as much the real need that people have for flower paintings. There are many of us who want to paint flowers in this way, and there is no reason whatever that with care in observation and materials, yours should not be successful. One of the reasons for the clarity and beauty of the original Dutch paintings was the great economic importance of flowers in seventeenth-century Holland. We have seen that Dutch painting reflected most aspects of their world, and flowers were among them. Tulips were marketable commodities and vast sums were exchanged for bulbs. It is even recorded that one merchant sold his house for a single bulb. It is not surprising that the pretty tulip appears so often in paintings. Looking at a beautiful Dutch flower painting it is tempting to think that there are secrets of the art. One never gets anywhere by looking for secrets in any branch of art or science, so let us look for the obvious. To a large extent the Dutch painters were the most meticulous craftsmen, many artists having come to painting via craftsmanship. If we take care from the beginning with fine craftsmanship it sets us off to a good start.

The craft of fine flower painting. Assuming that you are

painting on board, you will need a board that has been sized and has at least two coats of white priming but to be certain there should be three. It is an opportunity, if you like, to use a circle, oval or any other out-of-the-ordinary shape that takes your fancy. You should use lead or titanium priming, rather than acrylic; acrylic is a bit inclined to be slippery. The ground should be quite smooth. If needs be, the ground should be gone over with fine sandpaper. If you look at an original Dutch painting, and I mean an original, not a good reproduction, you will often see a dark, even black, background. This does not mean you should then cover the ground with black paint. If you do, you will get an immediate effect by painting the flowers on top of that, but in a very short time their colours will darken disappointingly. A thin glaze of raw umber can do no harm, and if the white of the board is formidable then give a *thin*, well-diluted glaze of raw umber. *Thin* is emphasised as a thick layer of underpainting will mean that any subsequent layer will sink; and it is always good to begin any oil painting by starting thin and working up thicker.

Beginning to paint the flowers. Most probably Dutch flower paintings were from accurate drawings. It is more than possible that Dutch artists kept drawings in their studio for use in all their paintings. This is a perfectly reasonable method. The drawings themselves would need to be as meticulously accurate as the botanical drawings described in the last chapter. If you were highly skilled you could paint flowers directly from life. But as painting in the Dutch style implies slow and meticulous workmanship you may, of course, find you have not completed the flower before it has died on you. The only way you can find out what is for you is by trying, and not minding if your first efforts go hopelessly wrong. Though if you really are a timid beginner perhaps you had better work from drawings. This will give you the extra advantage of being able to fit flowers of different seasons all into the same picture.

Designing the picture. The design of carefully painted flower paintings is of vital importance. In the bad ones the artist has painted a perfectly reasonable portrait of single flowers, but their arrangement, one to another and to the whole area of the board, has scarcely been considered. If you are thinking we come back inevitably to the design of drawings, we do, it is unavoidable. So here goes.

1. Make a series of accurate drawings in pen and ink or pencil. It would be an idea to tint your drawings with colour to remind you of the real colours, and/or add the pattern of shadings. *Drawings* please, photographs will *not* do. Choose either your favourite flowers, or flowers of a favourite colour. Another idea is flowers with a theme, like entirely dried plants of winter and autumn. You could, like Jan Breughel de Velours, even put flowers in for their symbolic language. The drawings then have to be composed into a painting. This may seem like a self-conscious artifact but once you make any decision on a canvas it is a self-conscious artifact. Only things like petrol patterns on a wet road are not. So next:

2. Set up your drawings in a row so that you can see them.

3. On a piece of paper draw in reduced scale the exact shape of your board, about 15 x 10 mm. Draw several shapes; this does not have to be on expensive paper.

4. Then, within each shape vary the shapes of the combinations of your flower drawings till you get something that is more pleasing than less. I do not say absolutely pleasing, or else you may experiment for ever, never committing yourself to a drawing for the finished painting. Do not forget the give and take of the relationship of the spaces between the flowers, that is, the shapes they leave out (Fig. 58). When you have decided remember that you can change the arrangement of leaves to effect the most pleasing design. Do not forget a jug for the flowers, and this too can be a drawing from anything that appeals to you. Or else, as many Dutch painters have, overcome the problem of showing the jug by covering the area with leaves, etc. To be more accurate, the 'etc.' in many Dutch paintings were various things connected with horticulture such as snails, butterflies, even snakes and hedgehogs. Please yourself.

5. Then to transfer the drawing to your board. You can do this by squaring up or by eye, free-hand. When you draw in paint on to the board, use thin paint. The flowers should be clearly outlined in either viridian or raw umber well diluted, or in between the flowers, thinner washes of colour.

6. *To paint.* You are discovering by now that a certain sort of patience is essential for this sort of work, using a careful and

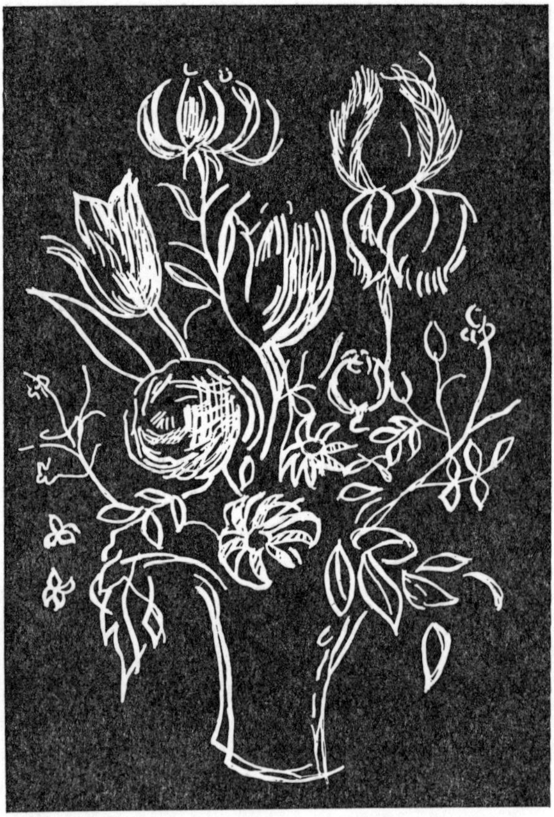

FIG. 58 *Set-piece flower paintings depend on design of the whole picture and good spacing between individual plants.*

deliberate craftsmanship. You should aim to carry out the whole painting like this. Thin, limpid paint is essential for this work. If you are painting thinly from start to finish the oil can evaporate leaving the paint surface looking dull. This is discouraging, so to avoid this add stand oil instead of linseed oil, or, in the usual turpentine/linseed mixture add a few drops of copal medium.

7. *Next – brushes.* For fine work the very choicest sable or kolinsky. These never leave behind brush hair marks (which in themselves are attractive in other techniques of painting) and are good for applying paint on paint without disturbing underlayers.

8. First cover all the areas of the board in approximate colours to the correct shapes. *All* the board. If you get so carried away

by the flowers only, you will never fit the background round them to make them look right.

9. There may be every reason to refer to a real flower rather than your drawing, so bear in mind to do so.

10. Once you have started with good drawing design, then the hard struggle is over. Tonality is important to the design of any picture. To make the flowers clear and stand out the background has to be much lighter or much darker. In a dark background you can make the flowers recede into it by gently blurring the wet paint.

11. In fact, background colour is important. I prefer the darker neutral ones, but you have anything you please. Blue gives the emotional impact of distance and remoteness, and may suit the mood of the painting. Then there is green that suggests vegetation.

12. We are thinking in terms of thin paint. To keep its clarity and transparency, at all times go steady with white. Only mix with white where really necessary and then in minimal quantities. Remember that greens can be lightened by yellows. In any case you will be using yellows to make greens warmer, so there may be no need to use white at all. If you are sparing with white when you do use it, it has all the greater impact. You will notice that some Dutch paintings are finally adorned with glistening water drops where the brilliance of the white shows up on darker leaves. For a beginner this habit of trying to make a painting glitter could be dangerous. If you add water drops, do so by observing real ones on real leaves.

13. Thin paint also suggests the delightful possibility of glazing. This, as we have seen before, is laying entirely transparent paint over another colour so that the under-painting just shows through the glaze. You can get some unusual colours. Here are some suggestions for transparent glazing colours. Quinacridones, magentas and pinks glaze particularly well over blues, whites and orange. Viridian glazes well over blues and yellows. Monestial or thalo colours are very intense, while they make unusual glazes, use them thinly. They become a bit harsh if glazed over plain white, and are best glazed over a warm colour.

14. Just a warning. No amount of accurate details of plants added bit by bit will make a good picture if the fundamental drawing is unsound.

15. 1–14 was one approach to meticulous plant painting. It may seem too laborious to some artists so to follow here are some other ways of going about it.

16. You may have a natural facility. Something in your hand obeys your eye-brain without too much to impede it. Facility need not be related to the selective and analytical process of your eye-brain, and how happy for artists when it is. If you have not natural facility remember the great painters who have overcome the lack of it, Constable, Cézanne, Poussin. If you have facility remember the many artists it has destroyed. But, you have the facility. In this case you could probably paint from live flowers directly on to the board. Naturally you should have a good idea of the design of your picture. It would then be sensible to paint each flower in turn.

17. To paint live flowers quickly and effectively with each successive layer of paint on top of a dry one, you should use the new gel painting media. These are thixotropic, the more they are brushed about the more fluid and thin they become. They are described in detail on page 31.

18. Naturally if you work from everlasting flowers or dried flowers you need not make drawings to paint from and you can work directly from the plants.

Another approach to flowers. You respond to flowers. We all do. Your instinct to paint may not be towards meticulous recording of flowers, on the contrary, brightly coloured flowers may make you feel excited and free. It is you, the way you feel, and this is about your painting. So supposing you do want to express the liveliness and gaiety of flowers in the way that the aged Monet's *Lily Pond* and Bonnard's paintings appear to. I say 'appear' as Monet's late paintings were the result of sixty years of painting and Bonnard was the most deliberate of painters. You could go ahead and paint, letting yourself go with paint on board. This might be a great deal of fun, painting frenziedly, involved with the paint and canvas. Then you stand back to see what you have painted, you now consciously alter or take out or put in what makes the picture look better. Perhaps you will just paint mixing colour, splashing it on, and the result will be expression of the feeling of the flowers (Fig. 59). Your painting will be a reminder, an atmosphere of flowers, even if a botanist would not call it accurate representation.

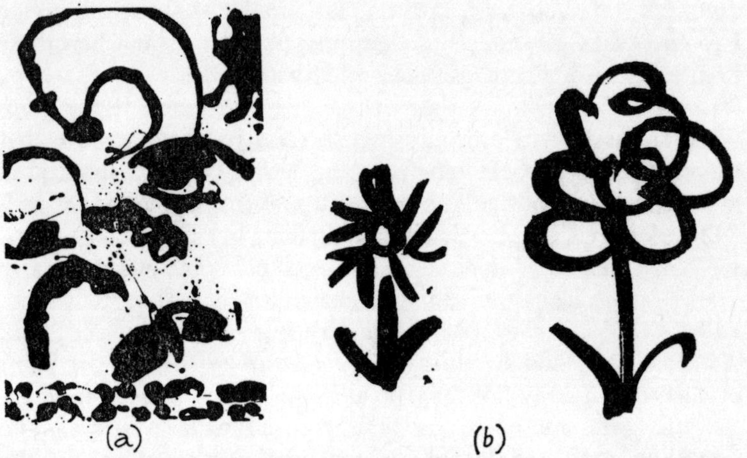

FIG. 59 *Painting from paint.* (a) *A Jackson Pollock painting, 1951.* (b) *Flowers from paint.*

All of us at some time have been pleased by seeing and painting flowers in this way. It is one of the more delightful characteristics of children's paintings. Freely painting flowers should be done with largish brushes using medium thin paint. You can use paint directly from the tube, without medium, but this is not only very expensive, but also liable to make the surface crack. Painting as you feel is good for every painter at some stage. The painting should be left when it is just at the point where it is what you want, there is no compulsion to go on. Is spontaneous painting unselfconscious? Is any painting unselfconscious? For little children's and even monkeys' paintings are taken from them when the effect pleases the teacher or keeper. Unselfconsciousness in art is almost impossible to define. What seems a freely handled painting can be the result of years of patient exercise that has become part of the eye, brain and hand of the painter. Processes, like all learning, once learned cannot be unlearned. So this brings us to the next point. How long can an artist paint freely without needing to learn more? The answer is, of course, that you can splash paint about for as long as it gives you pleasure, and gives other people pleasure too. Many beginners start painting by splashing on colour, and why shouldn't they? Not many beginners can continue getting, quick, cheerful paintings; if you can, go on for as long as it is giving happiness and pleasure. But there may come a point when these first, untutored efforts lose their vitality and original forte, having exhausted the limited resources that inspired them. If this happens, as more than probably it will, then you have to face that the first stage of beginning is over. Now you have to acquire knowledge consciously. The immediate results of this, be warned, will make your paintings not free at first, but more constricted. Do not think now that all is lost and that you ought to give up. At your most difficult moment this is the time to go on, as it is the only way you can absorb new-found knowledge till it becomes as though natural. So to return to the specific point of cheerful, splashy flowers – do as many as you please but when the fun goes out of it, recharge yourself with exercises. The preceding may have implied manipulating the paint on the board, a perfectly good way to paint. The other extreme is thin, transparent areas of paint diluted with turpentine only. To keep the transparency, do not use any white with the colours. But if transparency is to be kept, then this prohibits much over-painting. This technique is admirable for quick, brilliant effects, but be warned, in large quantities it will be very extravagant with boards!

As much as starting off with bright, splashy flowers, the reverse process may be so. Your work may be small, painted from the wrist rather than the arm. Of course, small, meticulous work may be the way you, by nature, paint, it *is* you. But it might be a very good thing if every so often you loosened up your work by painting freely with your arm. It is almost essential for painters who habitually paint on a small, almost miniature scale, to paint large.

Towards abstraction. The idea of cheerful, splashy flowers can lead into the next development, another approach to abstraction. A reasonable generalisation about the sources of abstraction is to say that there are two. One, the clear linear abstractions of Mondrian that evolved from cubism. The other came from paint. The Asiatic Russian, Kandinsky, d. 1944, who gave the first formal theory of abstraction, relates that he came into his studio and was suddenly struck by the beauty of the chance mixture of colours on the palette, lovelier than the calculated painting on the canvas. This was the seed of the idea of painting from paint, becoming intensely involved with the paint itself without reference to the external world.

Paintings from paint. For some beginners this may be a very good way to start you painting. Especially if you are a bit afraid of painting and dread making a mess of a subject picture. You start off by not minding if the painting is a mess, so cannot get worse. You will also learn a fair amount about the feel of paint, referred to before, and almost certain to be referred to again. Painting is a physical action and all good oil and water colour painters have a sensuous, even sensual understanding of oil paint. The greatest (or if you do not think they are great, the most significant) artists who followed Kandinsky were the American abstract expressionists, to be closely followed by the French tachistes. Of the Americans, Jackson Pollock's work has extraordinary vitality and intensity. Gentler and more lyrical are the paintings in stains of transparent colour by Sam Francis.

So to begin using your paint. Your board and your paints. If all the colours are a bit alarming restrict yourself to either the earth colours or any other limited palette. Having mentioned Jackson Pollock you might like to trail paint over the canvas surface taking it where the paint itself decides to go. Here comes a difficulty. You cannot do this in artists' oil paint whatever medium you mix it with. To make paint trail in lines you have to use decorators' out-door, high-gloss, oil-based paint. *Not* thixotropic drip. Probably, at home, you have discovered that decorators' paint trails just when you do not want it to. Be warned though, decorators' paints for this purpose are not permanent. This does *not* mean in terms of one hundred years, it means five or ten. But, you are warned, and if the idea looks like fun go ahead. Alas though, many of Jackson Pollock's highly original paintings are in a hopeless condition. If asked I would recommend that you stick to oil paint.

So on with painting. It is quite simple; just get started and the worst is over. While you are not sticking to formal or academic rules of design, it is as well not to be too haywire with your materials. Stick to the usual procedure of starting thin and working up thickly, or don't and do not blame the result in ten years on me. Respect your materials and equipment at all times. Remember you would if cooking or ponies were your hobby. This *is not* conceit. What is conceit is imagining your *one* masterpiece, just one painting, will astound the world and make you famous. I hope it does but it will not. So once more back to the board, a hog hair brush, media and paint. What colour appeals to you? Any colour? Dip into the colour with your brush, some medium and paint some sort of shape. Don't be timid, just paint, paint the shape somewhere in the canvas, but it had better not be in the middle. Your shape painted, rinse your brush. With any colour, or even the same one, paint another shape just as you feel. A shape to balance or complement, or just a shape. This is so personal that my diagrams do not help much beyond saying they are mine and yours are yours. Keep going. Do not worry that things may go wrong. If they go wrong paint them right. You can either paint away for a half an hour or more and then stand back to see what you have painted, or stand back continually as you paint. By the first process you can find you have accidentally painted some very exciting things, colours, shapes and tones. But your conscious decision makes you play around with the accidental effects. Try taking out whole passages of painting, if you want to, with a palette knife or, for that matter, rub in the paint with a palette knife. This leads to . . .

Painting with a palette knife. The very agreeable sensation of pasting slabs of paint on to the board. If you are concerned with permanence then see that the slabs of paint are not too thick, certainly no more than a millimetre. It might be as well in any case to mix some bees-wax medium with the paint or thixotropic gel. While I have found an ordinary palette knife perfectly good for painting, real addicts might like to use a flexible painting knife specially manufactured for this. The flexible knives are not much good for rubbing in paint; here you are better off with an ordinary palette knife. Smoothing out paint blurs outlines and makes an agreeable surface for glazing, but you have to let the paint dry first.

The texture of paint. We are considering the sort of painting where the texture of the paint, even of every individual colour, is part of the quality of painting. Colours have their individual textures, opacities and transparency. It might be fun to extend this by giving paint a conspicuous texture. At risk of impermanence you can set about sticking small objects in thick paint just as it takes your fancy. One has seen amusing assemblages of things stuck in paint. A curious aspect of twentieth-century art, that what to one person is waste, to another is an art object. A very usual thing to impale on to a wet paint surface is old watch wheels, they always look pretty. Though once you go in for this sort of thing there is no stopping you. A way of effecting texture is to mix sand with paint. This, by the way, is ruinous for brushes, so only use very old brushes. Another technique dependent on texture . . .

Sgraffito, a word applied to wall scribbles. The amount of

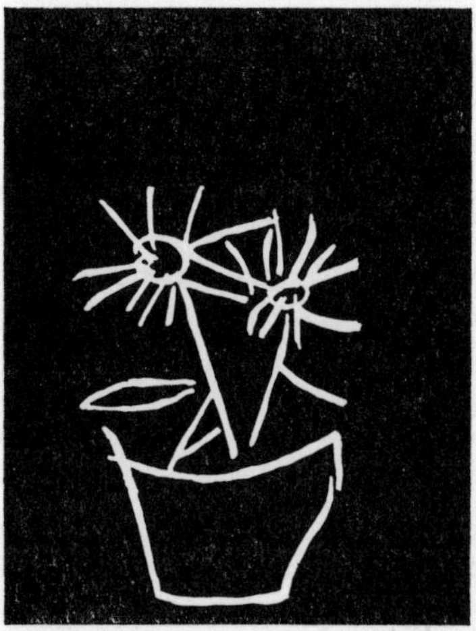

FIG. 60 *Sgraffito – its effect depends on the jerky awkward lines.*

contemporary interest in this cannot be entirely dismissed as a fad. Scratching at a surface to draw is satisfying. For a painting, put paint on with a palette knife in thin slabs. Wait for the paint to dry for over a week then cover over with a thin coat of contrasting tone, say brown on white, or cream over red, till the undercoat is obscured. Then, with the wrong end of the brush, scratch a drawing through the top coat (see Fig. 60).

To start out painting with paint is like starting out on an adventure journey with no deliberate end, being pleased with the unexpected things that turn up on the way, changing your mind and turning back too. Even if you start a painting with the most carefully planned drawing, do not forget that accidental discoveries may make it worth abandoning your original idea. We started the chapter with pretty and pleasing flowers, and have come a long way from that.

To return to flowers and another approach to flowers. You might say just painting flowers because they are pretty and pleasing is reasonable enough. In any really pretty picture there has to be an element of seriousness. One is intensely aware of this in the culture of France. There are decorative paintings of ornaments, cartouches and pretty clothes that have an unmistakable element of fine line, proportion, clarity and restraint. So remember this when, with your paint and canvas, you try to capture *La Rose en Sa Belle Jeunesse!*

Here we can look at the techniques of oil painting that fall somewhere between the meticulous and the entirely free. That is, the suggestive brush stroke. The ambivalent brush stroke that is somewhere between the purely drawn lines is almost a blodge, and yet, at a distance, becomes an image we read as form. The examples are many, Velasquez being the master of this type of paint handling. Perhaps no book can entirely tell you how, for can a book give you basic sensibility and judgment? But we will try. A handful of flowers in a vase, just as they are, no need for formal flower arrangement here (Fig. 61). Your paints, your medium.

1. Cover all the canvas with basic colours in thin paint.
2. Another layer to bring out the forms. Do not get stuck entirely on the flowers.
3. You have not done a preliminary drawing? The shapes may now need a bit of pushing about and altering.
4. How, though, to effect paint as flowers? Gently put the paint on, as Renoir said: 'Caress the canvas.'
5. Paint is flexible – push it about. Stand back – do you read an equivalent for a flower? Yes? Well and good.
6. No? Try another flower. Merge the paint a bit with the background. Put on more paint, move it about, make experiments with brush marks. Keep standing back, this is important as we are concerned with the mechanics of your eye resolving an image. As soon as the image appears, right, leave it.
7. None of this is to be confused with the adding of glittering highlights. If anything the lightest parts should be worked in as

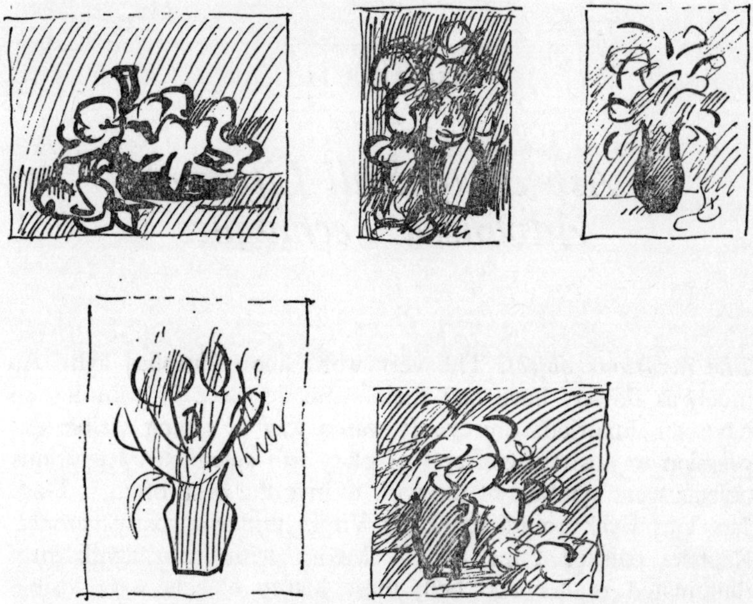

FIG. 61 *You may want to paint a simple vase of flowers. Here are some classic compositions.*

you go.

8. Eventually you have a painting of the object in the external world. If the flowers or anything else appeal to our senses of sight and touch so too should their recreation in terms of paint.

Wash brushes – clean your palette!

CHAPTER II

Aspects of Still Life and Advanced Techniques

The luxurious object. The very word luxury implies light. As much as flowers have had their symbolic place in painting, so have the luxurious objects. It was a way of giving visible expression to abstract concepts of glory and splendour. Luxurious objects were symbols of the wish to give the best, often to God. Jan Van Eyck paints the Holy Virgin under a costly coronet. Raphael painted Pope Leo X Medici with his magnificently illuminated psalter and bell; these luxury objects were visible symbols that the church was to have the best. The very fact that the artist has painted them is some tribute to the artist, that his eye, hand and paint gives them greater immortality still. Maybe when wealthy Dutch merchants commissioned artists to paint their fine possessions, the art work suggested a level of immortality, a symbol of the spiritual that the original gold or silver did not have. I have yet to see a really good modern painting of the luxurious objects of stateliness and refinement we see in the old Flemish and Dutch paintings; it may be that we are living in more matter of fact times. Very few people today have that curious mixture of love for the material and spiritual that characterised the Italians of the Renaissance and the Dutch of the seventeenth century. Since the nineteenth century, break-away movements from the academies developed a horror of paint imitating textures or surfaces. This is an understandable reaction against the glossy, overworked finish of high Victorian art. Hence you see the developments in the still life, especially those of Braque, of the paint's texture for its own sake. More recent paintings in the surrounds of 'pop art' have returned to mimicking surface texture. The attitude is rather implying that the viewer is familiar with photographs, and the artist is making a joke of this. To return, though, to the art of the past, a time when lives, even of the rich, were dingy, dull and disease ridden. The luxury object was the rarity, for only things that were expensive reflected light clearly as light fell on them; gold, silver, jewels and fine glass. No wonder they became symbols of light in the theological sense. In our present age of cheerful synthetics, cheap glass, when most people look jolly and nice, this symbolism has vanished. But past or present you, yes, you, and no one else may want to paint a picture of fine possessions and it is what *you* want to do that the book is about. So what if gold or silver or lace has to be transformed into its equivalents in oil paint? What amounts to . . .

Oil paint as equivalents to light and shadow. In the seventeenth century, a great age of still life painting, light and dark expressed a whole interpretation of the universe, it cannot do that today, but this does not prevent us learning from these paintings. The simple facts of light and dark in oil paint are that dark tones are transparent and light ones opaque. But this is not enough to teach you to paint a still life.

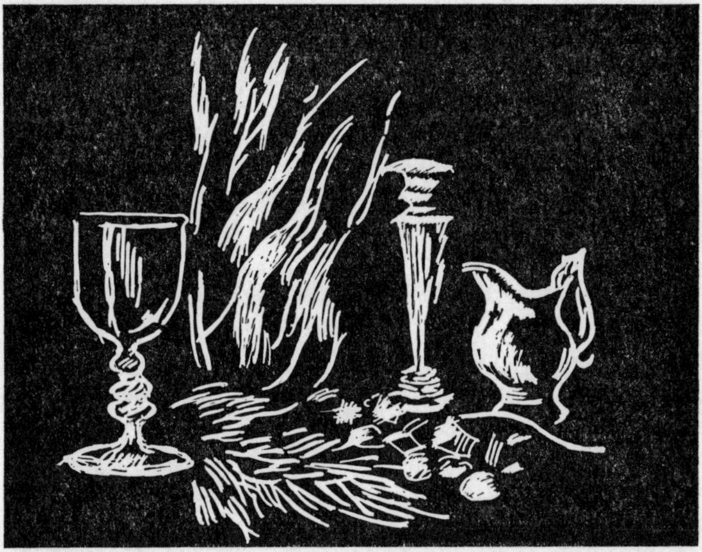

FIG. 62 *We see luxurious objects by the way light falls on surface. Hard lights for glass, metal and gems; softer lights for textiles.*

Arranging a still life. Your precious and beloved objects, and light. The effectiveness of light on surface is best expressed by contrast to shade so be very careful how the light falls on your objects. The light should be consistent and not changing, and preferably daylight. Use your discretion, for darks should not be too dark so that the colour is taken out of the objects. The objects should be contrasted with a drapery or background that shows them up to best advantage (Fig. 62). In arranging the still life you can, if you enjoy this sort of thing, indulge any feelings you have for texture. Look around you for luxurious textures. What can you see? Jewels? Silver, gold, damasks? Of course this does not preclude any other subjects we have studied – plants, flowers, rare fruits, like those you see in the beautiful Dutch paintings. On the subject of the Dutch still lifes, when you look at them you will see that they seldom use anything other than a straightforward technique with sable brushes. This is an area of painting where our sense of touch is not only related to our response to paint and canvas, but related to our sense of sight. We see, then we want to touch.

To start painting. There is something in many people's nature that likes adding white highlights at the end, just to give dull painting a sparkle. Well, it is a bit more complicated than this.

The picture has to be designed and drawn. Tonality is very important in this case and you should do a tonal sketch. You may also need to make several detailed drawings of the individual objects so as to get to know them (Fig. 63). This will give you a measure of facility, I do not say slickness, when

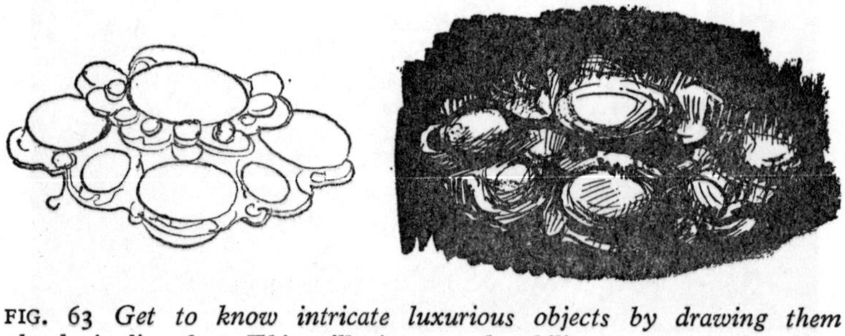

FIG. 63 *Get to know intricate luxurious objects by drawing them clearly in line first. This will give you the ability to suggest the object by light on surface.*

you come to the actual painting. Nothing whatever can be gained by struggling on with useless difficulties. But now you will come across an interesting problem. If you do an outline drawing of an object how can this relate to a recreation of light in terms of a brush stroke? An outline drawing at any time is a marvellous discipline for the artist and in an outline all is revealed and no weakness can be disguised, and you should do one. But you could also do a tonal drawing in pen and ink, which will relate more immediately to the kind of strokes you make with brush in paint.

To paint. In extensive use of darks remember when the oil dries it has a discouraging habit of looking duller than when it was wet. There are three ways round this: putting up with it, and then adding a final coat of varnish after the painting is finished; adding a few drops of copal to your turpentine and linseed oil; and the third is using thixotropic painting gel as this brings a very high gloss. Leaving white bits of priming showing through your painting is not going to help you at all, so be sure that your first thin layers of paint cover *all* areas of the board. To effect the greatest contrasts between darks and lights try to see that as little white as possible lightens the darks. I do not say none, but remember the following earth colours are lighteners as well as white. They are:

Flesh colour – a sort of terracotta pink ;
Naples yellow; and
Yellow ochre.

At the other extreme do not dip into black all the time, only use black when you want a truly intense dark. If you use it the whole time you will have no real extreme. (This is like folk who devalue adjectives of praise by continual use.) Here are some ways of getting some very intense darks without using black:

Synthetic indigo, plain, unmixed.

Monestial or thalo green + violet gives a dark, deep, cold, neutral transparent glaze. Mixed again with raw umber it is almost black.

Monestial + violet + light red gives a dull, sombre grey.

Raw umber is a sympathetic, neutral warm darkener of the bright colours.

Black is an extreme cold darkener of bright colours.

There are now several organic-dye dark browns on the market that are permanent and excellent.

Texture and light. We recognise a texture by the way light falls on it. Looking immediately around you, what do you see? Look very carefully; there may be glass, your woollen jumper, some unpolished wood, apart from the objects of the still life. Does it look unsurmountably difficult? Because it isn't really. Many things that *look* difficult are really quite easy when you have a go. It is the simple standing nude figure where your difficulties will begin. In the drawing (Fig. 62) you see a candlestick in the still life. So it is quite simple. With sable brush dipped in thin white paint you draw the *shape* of the light on the candlestick, and you have created texture and form. Now

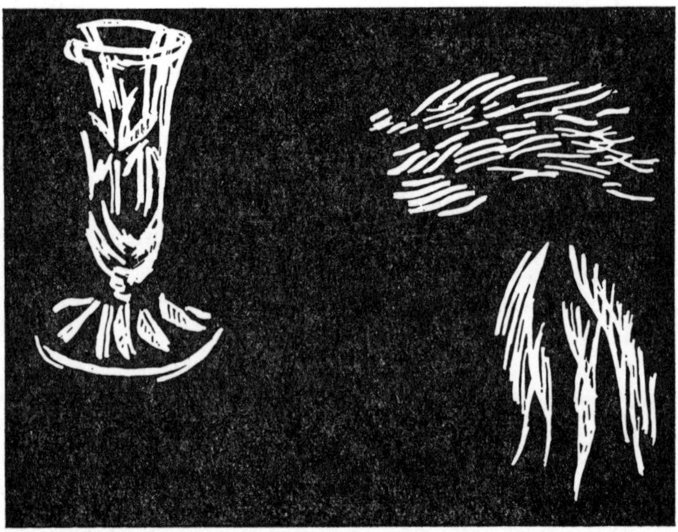

FIG. 64 *The texture of the goblet is recognised by the way light falls on it.*

the goblet and the same process (Fig. 64). Take a careful look at the velvet. The light is falling in little tiny soft specks, fading away softly at the folds. Not difficult to recreate with a sable brush.

To work further into the picture. Now stand back and you will find the picture is not finished by any means. The white highlights may look dreadfully bright, destroying the quality of the colours you have already painted. Or you may find the darks are not so dark but are lighter. Don't panic or do anything drastic. Gently does it. You may have to scrape down a bit with your palette knife if the paint has got too thick and this may unify the colours. Very likely you will find that you will have to reduce the range between the lightest tone and the darkest. Too violent contrasts between lights and darks in paintings are inclined to cancel each other out. So the whites in your painting may have to be scraped down and repainted, lowering their tone. Look carefully at the highlights, are they cold lights? If so they will have to be gently toned down with blue. If they are warm, then with ochre. It is easy enough to tone down lights. It is a bit more tricky to lighten extreme darks. The thing you must *not* do is frantically add whites to the darks; you will only get a dull, heavy mess. Scrape down a dark that is thickly painted. Then remix the colour, adding any other light earth, not white, to begin with, only adding white if you have to. If the painting has gone drastically wrong, no doubt you know the classic technique. In the words of Sir Tom Monnington P.R.A., '*Let the painting paint itself*'. This means putting the picture away for a week, at least, the longer the better, and then turning it face upward, coming to it quite fresh. You will find that your painting looks more different than you ever thought it would. A bit better here, a bit worse there, but unexpected. Now hang the painting up where you cannot escape seeing it; keep looking at it for about a week and suddenly it will dawn on you exactly what to do. The more fanciful among you could call this inspiration, but inspiration only comes from hard work you have *done*, not towards exciting things you hope to do. So in a way, the painting, an autonomous universe, tells *you* what to do. You may need some of the more advanced techniques listed below.

This is a beginner's guide, so by separating techniques it is to define them clearly, not to make you think that you cannot interchange them. Of course you can. Remember that a great professional master chef – and I do not mean a jolly good cook – learns a repertoire of classic teachniques before he invents the dishes that immortalise his name. An architect learns the basic classic orders before inventing a new one. For a painter then, here are some more classic techniques.

Stippling. It is a recognised technique. The fact that I think the effect quite horrid should not put you off! This means dabbing away with an old stump of a brush. It effects a broken up, not pleasant surface, though you may like it. Use an old brush, it will be ruinous to a new one. It is not to be confused with pointillism, which will be dealt with below.

Glazing. One of the most attractive aspects of oil painting is not only one's instinct to paste paint on, but to apply limpid, transparent glazes. Chapter 10 mentioned Sam Francis, the American, who built up a painting entirely in transparent glazes. The traditional and more usual method is to put a dark glaze over lighter, heavier under-painting. In the eighteenth century this was a usual technique for painting girls' pretty pink cheeks, though sadly, artists used fugitive colours, hence the palidness of the faces now. Renoir used this for that very purpose, as well as for flowers, fruits and backsides. It is essential to use permanent colours. Many colour manufacturers, especially 'Lefranc', list colours particularly suitable for transparent glazing. For glazing to be really effective the colour should *not* have any white or earth colour in it. Ideally glazes are best applied in single colours. In fact, the water colour techniques described in Chapter 9 are perfectly transmittable to glazing with oil colour. An oil paint glaze should be mixed with the usual turpentine/linseed mixture, and applied with any sort of brush. A glaze can be used to brighten any passage of a dull or dead painting. Of course you cannot glaze on wet paint. Glazes are best applied after two weeks. I suggest using a palette knife to scrape down rough edges before painting. If you want to glaze on a painting that has been dry for over three months, this is agreeable to do, but to ensure permanence first run over the surface well with turpentine. The new thalo (in Europe, monestial) and quinacridone colours are quite the best for glazing. In permanence they have vastly surpassed the traditional lakes, carmines and vegetable dyes. The exception is the soft, pretty terre vert. You can pleasingly glaze in any colour over white, and you could stick to this. But it is certainly worth being enterprising and trying to glaze colours on to mixed lighter colours, as you can get most subtle and unusual colours. It's very individual how *you* would go about it, but here are some ideas to start you off.

Thalo green (or monestial)	over orange
Thalo green (or monestial)	over light red
Quinacridone pink	over orange
Quinacridone pink	over cerulean
Manganese blue	over Naples yellow
Thalo violet	over light red
Terre vert	over yellow

Once a glaze has dried, again referring to the water colourists' technique, you can glaze even darker glazes over them again, letting some of the under-painting show through (Fig. 65). You can start a painting with deliberate intent to finish by glazing, as I have often done when painting flowers. Or you can glaze if a picture needs it. Very rich darks can be obtained by final glazes. Remember that glazes can go discouragingly dull, especially over darks. Final varnish (see end of chapter) will banish this and brighten the colours again. Read too page 174 about Chardin's methods of final glazing to unify a picture surface as this is a very good reason to glaze a picture.

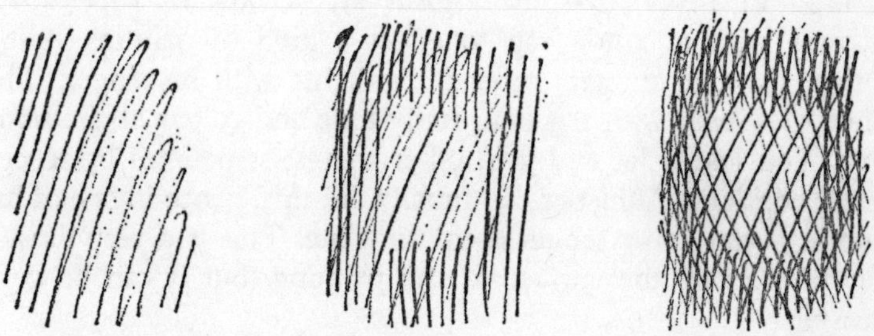

FIG. 65 *Glazing – this is very similar to water colour technique. It is running darker transparent colours over lighter.*

Scumbling. The opposite of glazing, though Renoir and quite different artists, e.g. Turner and Whistler, used bold scumbling and glazing in the same picture. To scumble then. This means to cover an area of painting with a thin, opaque glaze of white or a white-based mixture. Scumbling should not, unless you want it to, deliberately obliterate the paintwork it covers. The under-painting should just show through. To scumble with refinement requires the kind of sensibility that made a literary critic describe Coleridge as an epicure of words. Basically then, one scumbles with white. Chapter 2 discusses the different whites. As titanium white was not in use until the 1920s the finest scumble used was flake white. It is probably still the best. Flake white is the most transparent white, and in dilution will leave a warm milky glaze. I have never made a successful scrumble with zince white but you may be able to; flake white is better. If you intend to obliterate under-painting or do sgraffiti work (see page 149) then use titanium white. You will get a brilliant, cold film of white that will not go dead. The effect of scumbling is always to turn the under-painting colder. Indeed the *hotter* the under-painting and colder the effect of the scumble. A scumble over a red will appear bluish. Scumbling than can be used for its own sake or to cool passages of painting that are too hot. Some colours, greens, purples and blues, get paler after scumbling but do not, like reds, lose their identity. You can add the merest hint of colour to a scumble to vary it. Obviously a scumble is very good if you like adding highlights at the end as they are not too aggressive.

Wiping out – not to obliterate the painting entirely, of course. It used to be popular in English art schools to wipe down pictures with a cotton rag to effect a kind of painting unity. Titian, for that matter, rubbed highlights with his finger. The effect of wiping with rag is to unify tone and colour at the same time. You lose a lot and gain other things, sometimes by recognising accidents. Whistler continually did this, hence in one of his paintings you *never* see an absolute white. This is a very drastic way of treating the surface of the painting, but it can be very pleasing.

Transparent films of paint. The ultimate in abstract paintings with transparent paint is to float on the surface of the board enormous washes of paint dissolved in carbon tetrachloride. This is a solvent that sends off most dangerous fumes. Take care. Carbon tetrachloride is also very expensive. It dries immediately. Unless you can work out of doors and no expense is spared, this is *not* to be recommended. Though this in no way diminishes the marvellous abstracts painted by Paul Jenkins and Morris Lewis in this way.

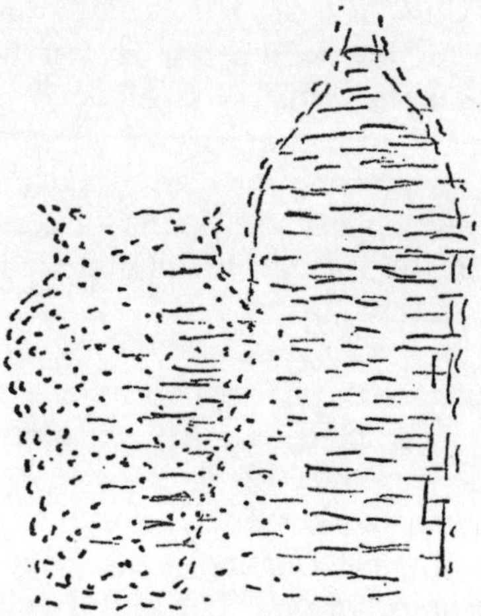

FIG. 66 *In pointillism there is no rigid outline. Colours reflect each other on separate objects and their opposites too.*

Pointillism. If you look at the surface of a painting by Seurat or any of his disciples, like Signac, you will see that it is covered by little dots (Fig. 66). It is more conspicuous in Seurat's disciples' work as it became rather a manner for its own sake. Seurat, as a painter, is a mystery. He tried to reduce painting to a science, as many have done before and since. He most resembles a scientist in his strange precocity. Seurat's symbols of the universe, like a mathematical prodigy, emerged ready-made. This may be suggesting that Seurat is inimitable. He is. But then imitation is never recommended and is not the same as true learning, any more than a clever mimic is a good actor. For all this you may like the effects of pointillism, which finally is every reason to do it. Pointillism is not a question of just dotting the paint on; if you feel like doing so with no further thought, go ahead and have fun. At a more serious level, pointillism is the logical conclusion of impressionism. The pointillists deliberately and logically took the current theories of Rood and Chevreuil to recreate light. The theory is that white light consists of all the seven colours of the spectrum, colours that take the opposite colour of those next to them and reflect back the same colour. Look at a real Seurat painting, *not* a colour reproduction, and you will see how he uses spots and dashes of colour to recreate light. He seldom mixes colour. The beholder's eye, at a distance, resolves the dots of colour into a unity. Not that this duality of vision is new, but Seurat's use of it is. What gives Seurat's paintings their power is that he relentlessly stuck to his theories, never deviating from them or from meticulous composition. His compositions are formal creations of a possible world. This probably sounds rather formidable, but it may be worth trying. Signac was Seurat's closest disciple, less rigorous and blandly colder than his master; it is obvious that he often used dot technique for fun because he enjoyed it. A good enough reason for us all.

Metallic colours. Jackson Pollock, often referred to in the text, uses metallic aluminium paint to great effect, but one is alarmed to think what a fearful legacy he may have left to some future restorer. We began the chapter with the luxurious object. Gold leaf was an ingredient of medieval panel painting if the patron chose to pay for it. Its symbolism is obvious. The joy of gold leaf on painting is that it can be burnished to shine, coming in very thin plates of beaten gold. Metallic paints are little tiny grains of metal suspended in the media. You *cannot* burnish or polish them. Gold paints are cheerful and lively for decorative work. But if asked, I would say, if you can afford gold leaf and the time to learn to apply it to gesso (plaster of Paris) ground, use it in fine art work, but do *not* use metallic paints as substitutes. Metallic paints go very dingy and could even turn black. Use metallic paints for fun but not much else. It is true that some metallic paints advertise themselves as being of quality. This refers to the fineness of the grains of metal in the paint.

Colour and expression. The quotations on page 178 from Matisse talk about colour and expression. You may not want to paint the colours of nature as they are, but as you feel about them. If you see a yellow in a flower it may make you feel you want to paint an intensified yellow. Looking at flowers on a tree against the sky, you may feel like painting the sky pink. Fruit in your painting you may want to be blue. There is nothing to stop you painting like this!

Difficulties. Mistakes you scrape out; difficulties are something else. Perhaps this should have been titled 'prevention is better than cure'. Remembering first that with any amount of research and care, there is always in painting an element of uncertainty. No handbook can give you fool-proof technique. But we can still look at difficulties.

'Sinking'. This is an advanced case of paint going dull. Thin paint goes dull. Thick paint can sink. The surface looks quite lifeless. The worst cause is bad priming and bad support, either too thin or too cheap, but worst of all is painting on to lead ground that has not dried thoroughly. If the cause is bad priming then, sorry, too bad, it is a hopeless case and do not let it happen again. If, as far as you know, the priming and support are sound then your case is curable. The most reliable way out I have found is to wait until the painting has dried, then rub the surface with a clean brush (*not rag*) with this mixture: $\frac{2}{3}$ linseed oil, $\frac{1}{3}$ turpentine, and a drop of dammar varnish. Rub the *whole* surface, even bits that have not sunk or else it will all go uneven again. For sinking many painters recommend . . .

Retouching varnish which will 'bring up' the surface of a painting immediately. The problem here is that many colourmen will not declare what *vernis à retoucher* contains, and the long term effects cannot be determined. If asked I would veto retouching varnish, though there are many who would not. This leads to . . .

'Secret' patent media. If there is a painting media that is secret, leave it. It will not be the elixir of life. Please yourself but I do not see that you can gain anything by trying to invent your own secret media, unless you have heirs who will record the results! To try to invent media is a waste of time.

Other difficulties. Paint surface wrinkling. This is caused by using thick amounts of cheap paint bound in too much oil and varnish. It can happen if any paint in one lot is over 2 mm thick. You cannot cure this.

Cracking paint. This may happen after a hundred years but should not after ten. Cause is usually not enough oil in the paint media.

Final varnishing. This seals and protects paintings and brings up the colour. Paintings should be left at least a year. Varnishing is not an arbitrary thing. It requires care. The old varnishes were made of dissolved resins or gums. The new ones are synthetic, expensive, but clear and excellent. When a picture is ready for varnishing and if it is on canvas:

1. Be sure canvas is stretched and pegged.
2. In any case try to varnish in a dust-free room.

3. Be *absolutely* certain *all* dust is wiped off the surface of the painting. Use a cotton rag.
4. Always varnish evenly with a large *soft* brush, it does not have to be an expensive one.
5. Consider the varnish coat as final. Never attempt to paint on top of it, or to work repainting into wet varnish.

Restoring paintings is not covered as this is far more a branch of chemistry than of fine art.

CHAPTER 12

Professionalism

Do not let this put you off. Perhaps a better title might have been 'a proper respect for your work place in the whole scheme of things'. St Thomas Aquinas once defined humility as a proper respect for one's place in the universe. So a respect for your profession or hobby is perfectly proper. Professionals are not versus amateurs, they complement one another. Many, even most, professional artists could learn a great deal from amateurs. They could learn from amateurs genuine love for the norms of the external world, flowers, children, landscapes, etc. Amateurs can learn the professional attitudes, regular work, and respect and care of equipment. Alberti, that great Florentine theorist of the quatrocento wrote that 'great arts arise from small beginnings'. It is possible that this noble humanist realised that many of the great arts of classical times, casting, building or decorating villas, etc., were passed down by ordinary people. Only out of the arts of ordinary people can we get the great arts. The cultural life of a society is as much measured by its amateurs. The amateurs paint often to please others, their family or friends. How many professionals have never achieved this! A subject worthy of the pen of Somerset Maugham would be the remorseless, dedicated artist wife who's hated her husband's work!

What we really mean by professionalism is selling; a two way thing. If you are the kind of artist who believes so intensely that you are a genius you will not need this chapter, as you will believe that it is people's duty to spend money on you. Most artists have a little more sensibility than this and even feel diffident about the whole business of money. Neither diffidence nor its opposite are very helpful to you as an artist so let us look at the whole problem in its various aspects.

Exhibiting. Still life and flowers stand a very good chance of getting into shows. Exhibitions are advertised in advance in all art journals. If there are rules for exhibiting obey them and do not try to think you will get away by being different.

A good frame and/or mount is important. You cannot take the risk of thinking that your creation is so supreme it will overcome a shoddy frame. It is well worth getting a good frame from an artist/framer who can see your work with an experienced eye. A good frame is *not* a waste of money and if need be can be used for several other paintings. *Price* for exhibiting work should include the frame. Don't ever underprice yourself. Here is a rough guide for pricing, measuring you up with other professionals:

10 x 20 cm approx. = $\frac{1}{8}$ of a professional's weekly earnings
20 x 30 cm approx. = $\frac{1}{4}$ of a professional's weekly earnings
40 x 60 cm approx. = $\frac{1}{2}$ of a professional's weekly earnings
80 x 90 cm approx. = a professional's weekly earnings

Let people pay for work. Never give work away, it will *not* be appreciated; if you do you are undercutting somebody who lives by selling. This does not mean that you should never lower your prices, you should, but use your judgement in doing so. A great deal of professionalism depends on using your instinct, and there are not any rules about this. Artists exhibit for three reasons: they want their work to be seen; they would like to sell; and finally, they want to get better as artists. The last is not least.

Exhibiting in a mixed show is a very good way of learning about your work and seeing it afresh, as your paintings have to hold their own in competition with others and you will find that feebleness and weakness show up at once. In public exhibitions there is usually a wide variety of work reflecting the varied tastes of a selection committee.

Private galleries. Here you are dependent on the taste of one or two proprietors. In the past, private galleries were often prepared to exhibit an artist whose work might not be popular but whom they believed had merit. In these days of soaring rents and rates in cities, alas, this cannot be relied on anymore and nearly all dealers want to show work that they feel they can sell. This is not to put you off but to explain how things are. What cannot be alleviated but of necessity has to be gone through and is not agreeable is taking your work for a dealer to see. Colour slides are best for this. It is unlikely that the dealer will come to see you. Trailing your work round galleries is not pleasant. No dealer will behave before your work like Francia, who in 1517 collapsed and died before the beauty of a Raphael. The chances are that the dealer will find the fruits of your agony and ecstasy utterly mediocre. If he tells you to come back in two years because he is booked up, a good gallery should be, so advance booking is a sure sign that the gallery is reputable. Come back in two years. If the dealer asks for a couple of works for a mixed show this is a jolly good start, but ask for a receipt for them. A gallery that will not give you one is not worth dealing with. Consider yourself lucky if an experienced gallery owner is even interested enough in your work to criticise it. Listen carefully to what he says, it might be helpful. If a gallery proprietor shows even a glimmer of interest in your work, and is not too busy at that moment, ask for a criticism.

Price. If a gallery takes your work they will ask you to help them decide some sort of price, but remember they will take 33 per cent, so what with your cost of framing, do not leave yourself out of pocket. It is difficult for a struggling artist to remember that his relationship with a dealer is as an equal, so adopt from the first an attitude of equality as this is more likely to ensure reciprocal treatment. If you want to launch yourself locally with a one man show, try your public library or your local arts and crafts shop. Many universities and colleges have exhibition space and it is most rewarding to show in these.

Pay galleries. There are galleries where you can pay to show your work. In effect, you are renting gallery space. Sadly, in Britain, these galleries are not taken as seriously by the critics and connoisseurs as the galleries where the artist is *invited* to show work. This is rather unfair but that is how the matter stands. Somebody else may advise you differently but here is my advice. Only rent gallery space if you can afford it comfortably, and this means a slap-up private view party too. If it means pinching and scraping, a pay gallery in the U.K. is not likely to launch you. Don't try to paint pictures just to try to please the dealer unless he tells you; it is a waste of time. He will tell you soon enough if he wants them.

Critics. This can mean anybody from a highly-trained art

historian to any journalist scribbling the 'art' column because no one else is available. Good criticisms are encouraging, bad ones are beastly – it is as simple as that. It is strange that critics' opinions seldom affect actual sales. Most likely you will be ignored by critics. Should you ever find you admire the writing of any particular critic or value his opinion it is well worth writing a straightforward letter asking him to give an opinion on your work. If you advertise yourself as a genius (only you think you are) your letter will be ignored. The critic may tell you, perfectly truthfully, that however much he admired your work, his review may be crowded out for lack of space.

Studio visits. In the last century, artists often held open studio. It is not done very much now and is, perhaps, rather a loss. There are many people who might like to visit an artist's studio but feel that they would not know what to say, or worse, would not escape without being obliged to part with money. This now borders on the formalities of social behaviour which is not dealt with for the artist in any book I know, so it might as well be dealt with here. If you are the sort of artist who believes in 'sincerity' and 'truth' at all costs skip this, it is not for you; probably nothing is, except lavish compliments and even more lavish cheques.

Firstly for the artist. Remember the visitor to your studio is your guest first, a patron second. Have the place tidy and clean, though sparseness never matters. *Hide* whatever you do not want seen. Put out refreshments; *nice* refreshments, pleasingly done. If you *cannot* afford to, do without a meal the next day. It is disheartening the number of times you will not sell or have to live on your dainty sandwiches, peanuts and sherry for a week; but very probably the tax man will agree to your charging this to expenses. *Very few* visitors will rise above a place that looks messy and squalid, they will feel guilty and complicated and try to escape. Do not let your honoured guests freeze either. Don't *you* bring up the subject of buying, let your honoured guest do so. If they ask a price tell them frankly or, if you would rather, have a little hand-list ready with everything written. To us artists it is continually exasperating that nearly everyone has more money than we have, but this does not entitle us to expect people to spend it on us. Remember you are a professional and your good name for professional behaviour is very important. Somebody who has not bought your work but has enjoyed visiting your studio is a new friend and may very easily recommend you to others who do buy. *Do not ever* give your work away, not even for charity auctions. It will not be appreciated. As a general rule do *not* let people take work on approval, I have always been unlucky. About the fairy godmother, the rich patron who smilingly buys everything and makes you world famous; there is no such creature. Alas, for us all, only inspired drawing, tonality and colour can make us world famous. Finally, most of us, because we are artists, are sensitive and self-centred. Try not to take chance remarks uttered by your patron too personally. Easier written than done!

The patron visiting the studio. Remember the artist is a professional like a doctor or a lawyer. He is unlikely to be a jolly Bohemian as, indeed, few artists can afford to be. The artist is certainly poorer than you, so refrain, please, from saying that the oddly assorted china and furnishings are 'fun'; say nothing about them. The artist is *not* living like this for 'fun' and cannot have the way-of-life things that to you are essential and also taken for granted. If the artist says, 'Look at what you like,' he means it. If he does not, look at what he has put out and resist rooting around. If you are not used to looking at pictures familiarise yourself with art galleries and good paintings before visiting studios. Once you have bought a picture and handed over the money, that's that. If you change your mind that is your problem and on no account expect the artist to go back on the deal.

What to say – artist and patron. The studio, the private view. What to say? I believe it is perfectly reasonable to have a code of suitable expressions. There are going to be lots of artists who will say this is insincere. But wait a minute, artists – keep truth to your drawing. Remember the other person's sincere feelings may be, 'Your work is dead ordinary and I do not want to spend my money'. We do not want to hear that, so supposing we allowed our guests at the private view or the studio a code of etiquette. So for you, the patron, the visitor, it is perfectly acceptable, even if the paintings are not your type, to ask as many questions as you like about the artist's methods and materials. If you cannot make up your mind whether to buy or not, keep indecision to yourself. If you decide to, ask prices openly. Only your intuition will tell you if the artist can take criticism, though as a rule most artists cannot. If you, the patron, are invited to a private view, try to go. The more people the better, and the less likely, if you are unsure as to what to say, will you be put in a spot in an empty gallery facing the artist. For you, the artist, agreed private views are nerve-racking occasions and every remark made is painful, but remember the visitors are still your guests.

General. Keep photo slides of your work; catalogues where your work is numbered.

Commissions. Most usually flowers and still lifes are bought as they are. It is not usual that you will be commissioned to do a still life, but it could happen. In any case commissions can usefully be discussed. Of course, we come back to the two way artist/patron thing. There are artists who by their very nature cannot work to order and you may be one of them. Whether you can or cannot does not mean that you can or cannot paint. Many artists are conditioned by art-school teachers to believe that commissions lower your standards; nothing does that except bad drawing. If you are commissioned to do something name your price clearly, do not be tempted to lower it. If your patron wants, say, exotic fruit or flowers, he should be expected to pay for or provide them. If, by ill luck, you find you are landed with a patron who is continually dissatisfied or, with the best possible intent on both sides, the commission does not please, do not make scenes, settle reasonably for a quarter of the original agreed price. Extensive and large commissions, say, anything over £100 in agreed price or your expenses, should be confirmed in writing. Those over £300 should have expert advice and a contract. Banks would consider these seriously if you wanted an overdraft. For expert advice see below. If you are business-like from the start this will set a good workman-like atmosphere for painting and discourage defaulters.

Artists' Information Registry, Burlington House, Piccadilly, London, W.1. This admirable institution keeps a photo slide register of artists' work. This is for people to consult who may want to place a commission with almost any sort of artist. It also publishes a news-sheet of forthcoming events, exhibitions, competitions and a list of addresses useful to artists. The Artists' Information Registry will also put you in touch with lawyers who specialise in artists' problems. Most capital cities have institutions of this kind and here is a list of some of them.

PARIS	Centre National d'Art Contemporain, 11 Rue Berger, Paris 8. Library and archive centre on contemporary artists with visual documentation.
FLORENCE	Centro. Publishes bulletin. Library of visual documentation.
U.S.A.	Washington International Arts Letter, 1155 S.E. Washington DC. A letter service and digest concerning twentieth-century patronage, support programmes.

Amateur/professional. In the artist's life these are not easily divided. Very often artists augment their income from their creative work by teaching or something else. Many amateurs spend more time on their art than so-called professionals. It is a question of attitude. Assume a professional attitude and you will be treated as a professional.

Provenance. When you sell work the buyer should have a provenance. This is the painting's pedigree. The following information should be on a label stuck on the back of the picture. This helps the owner's insurance and, should you ever become famous, will enormously help art historians.

Artist's name.
Date of painting, e.g. 1973.
Title of painting, e.g. *White Roses.*
Exhibited, e.g. Paris Salon, 1974.
Published information, e.g. Paris Salon catalogue critique in *Daily Echo* and in *Literary Review.*
Other information, e.g. drawing for same published in *Art.* Similar painting in the collection of Oxbridge University gallery.

Some more practicalities if any students are reading this. If annoying people ask you what you are going to do when you leave art school tell them you are going to paint and don't be apologetic. You are going to. At first, you are going to take any commission that comes your way rather than not paint at all. Before you know where you are you will be making some money. When the happy day comes when half your money comes from painting, you are doing pretty well, over half and you are home and dry. At first you may have to teach. Your students and pupils are going to have far more respect for a teacher who does have a professional practice.

Plant drawing. May I point out that if anyone can do fair, competent, clear plant drawings then this can lead you to getting work at various scientific institutions, where this sort of drawing is always in demand.

CHAPTER 13

Other Painters Say . . .

Throughout the text it has been emphasised that your real teachers are the great masters of the past, whose work has stood the test of time. Here now are quotations mostly from and about still life painting and still life painters but some others too. There are no apologies for twice quoting Constable in the text, not a still life painter, but so universal in attitude his remarks on painting could apply to any branch of the painter's art. The earliest references to flower and fruit painters occurs in Vasari's *Lives of Painters*. Pupils of Raphael are described as carrying out the beautiful garlands and arabesque decorations in the antique style that delights us to this day in the Vatican and the Villa Farnesina. Giovanni del'Udine and the other pupils of Raphael were never thought of as any more than excellent decorators, though at some later stage in history, a painter of this type would have become, as likely as not, a flower painter in his own right.

You should collect your own painterly notes, remarks of other painters on painting, favourite colour mixtures. Many painters collect inspiring passages from prose or poetry, or whatever else inspires their art. To begin then here is a description of the Dutch painter, *Jan de Heem,* who lived in Utrecht and Antwerp, his dates 1606–84:

'The famous artist Jan de Heem betook himself from his birthplace Utrecht to Antwerp because it seemed to him sensible, since one could have there rare fruits of all kinds, large plums, peaches, morellos, orange and lemons, grapes and others in finer condition and state of ripeness. He copied them with all kinds of flowers and other natural inanimate objects with exceeding excellence so that as is generally recognised, he surpassed all others in the Netherlands.'

Next, about one of the greatest of all still life painters, the French painter, *Chardin*, 1699–1779. Jean Baptist Chardin's paintings are a great contrast to the brilliant, fashionable paintings of Boucher, Lancret and Fragonard, though this did not prevent him enjoying great prestige in his lifetime and royal patronage. He showed regularly at the Paris Salon and was secretary-treasurer of the Academy. It is even said that Chardin intended to write a treatise on the colour white. The philosopher, critic and encyclopaedist Denis Diderot is quoted below on Chardin.

'It is always nature and truth. You will want to grasp the bottles by the neck if you happened to be thirsty, the peaches and grapes give you appetite and affect your fingers.'

'Ah Chardin, this is not white, not red, not black you mix on your palette, this is the every substance of the things, the air, the light you pick up on the point of your brush, and thence transfer to canvas . . . Approach and all looks confused, flattened and disappears, withdraw a little and everything reshapes itself and becomes present once more.'

Accounts by other contemporaries of Chardin:

'His pictures are silvery and vigorous, all the objects in them reflect each other and from this results a transparency of colour which enlivens everything his brush touches.'

'His colours, often enough are greyish. His manner of painting is unique. He puts on his colours one after another without mixing beforehand so that his painting looks like a sort of mosaic or a tapestry. He made use of a special glaze for the purpose of unifying his paintings.'

The engraver-secretary to the Academy, M. Cochin, describes this unifying glaze:

'Cologne earth, ashes of ultramarine, linseed oil. The finished picture should be gone over with these. It is necessary that the linseed oil should not be noticeable. I have heard M. Chardin say that with these tones differently mixed and modified, he went over all the dark parts irrespective of their colour. It is certain that he is the one painter of the age who understood the harmony of a picture.'

Gustav Courbet, 1819–77, was a magnificent and grand painter of the still life. He repudiated his contemporaries who were classicists or romantics, and was the first social realist. Much of his writing and activities were political but the passage below relates to his robust character in paint. Look at Courbet in the original and do not bother to read complex doctoral theses that look at him as a politician! From Courbet's manifesto, 1861:

'The art of painting should consist solely of the representation of objects visible and tangible to the artist . . . I hold also that painting is essentially a concrete art and does not consist of anything but the representation of the real and existing things. It is a completely physical language. Imagination in act is in knowing how to find the most complete expression of an existing thing, but never to suppose or invent that thing.'

Ingres, 1780–1867, was the leader of the classicists. His famous dictum, 'Drawing is the probity of art,' was parodied by his famous romantic rival Delacroix who said, 'Colour is the probity of art.'

Corot died ten years later than Ingres. He is best known for his landscapes but the following remarks contain such good sense about painting from nature, I feel it's worth including them.

'I am never in a hurry to reach details. First and above I am interested in large masses, and the general character of a picture, when these are well established then I try for subtleties of form and colouring. I rework the picture constantly and freely without any systematic method.'

'I profit from many lucky accidents.'

Vincent Van Gogh, 1853–90. One of the artists who has come into the popular consciousness more than any other. He has become a symbol for the artist who is poor and suffering in his lifetime, yet enjoys fame after his death, his pictures selling for astonishing sums. Yet, the story that has become the subject of two television plays, a Hollywood epic and a 'top of the pops' in no way should let us forget that Van Gogh was a relentlessly hard worker, whose only aim was to become a better painter. He was a highly intelligent man who read and spoke five major languages. Who cannot look now at a sunflower and not be reminded of Van Gogh? Surely this is the still life painter's greatest achievement, to make us see beauty where we would least think of finding it. Van Gogh's short and tragic life is revealed to us in letters he wrote to his devoted brother, Theo. From one written from Arles in 1888:

'It won't surprise you to know that what I'm at is the painting of some big sunflowers. I have three canvases in hand. The first, three huge blooms in a green vase with a light background, another against a blue background and the third twelve flowers and buds in a yellow vase.'

Gauguin was a contemporary and erstwhile friend of Van Gogh, he died in the Marquesas islands in 1903. His life too has become popularised, one fears for the wrong reasons. Gauguin has become the symbol of the stockbroker who ups and outs on western civilisation to paint. This alone is not enough to make you a good painter.

'What is sweeter to the artist than to make visible in a bunch of roses the tint of each one?'

'There is an impression resulting from any certain arrangement of colours, lights and shadows. It is what is called the music of the picture. Even before knowing what the picture represents, as when you enter a cathedral and find yourself at too great a distance to make out the picture – frequently you are seized by this magic accord. Here is the true superiority of painting over other forms of art, for this emotion addresses itself to the most intimate part of the soul.'

'Colour being an enigmatic thing in the sensations it gives us, can logically only be used enigmatically, every time it is employed, not for drawing, but for giving the musical sensations which proceed out of its own nature, its own interior, mysterious enigmatic force.'

Paul Serusier, who died in 1926, was a disciple of Gauguin in Brittany. He wrote an excellent theoretical treatise on painting which well deserves to be reprinted:

'The impression of nature must be wedded to the aesthetic sentiment which chooses arranges, simplifies, synthesises. The painter ought not to rest until he has given birth to the child of his imagination, begotten by the union of his mind and reality.'

Seurat, 1859–91, in his very short life produced a few but grand and compelling paintings. Never, in any of them, did he deviate from his theories of colour and harmony that were based in some degree on the Italian masters' system of proportion, but to a greater degree on the theories of his scientific contemporaries, Chevreuil, Rood, Sutter and Henry.

'Art is Harmony.

'Harmony is the analogy of contraries, the analogy of similarities in tone, colour and line considered under the aspect of the dominant one and under the influence of lighting in gay, calm or sad combinations. The contraries are . . . In tone, a lighter more luminous one in place of a darker, in colour, complementaries, that is, a certain red opposed to its complementary etc., red, green, orange, blue, yellow-violet in line those making a right angle.

'Gaiety in tone is through the use of dominant luminosity, in colour of prevailing warmth. In line those above horizontal.

'Calmness – tonally equality of light and dark, colour equality of warm and cool, in line the horizontal.

'Sadness, in tone dominant dark, colour prevailing cool, line downward from horizontal.'

Cézanne, 1839–1906, ranks with Chardin as one of the painters of the still life who, like Chardin before him, raised it to the level of a great classic form of expression and analysis. In his old age he wrote a series of letters to Emil Bernard setting out his theory of painting.

'May I repeat what I told you, treat nature by the cylinder, sphere and the cone, everything in proper perspective so that each side of an object or a plane is directed towards a central point. Lines parallel to the horizon give breadth, lines perpendicular to the horizon give depth. Nature for us men is more depth than surface.'

'An optical impression is produced on our organs of sight which makes us classify light half tone or quarter tone, the surfaces represented by colour sensations.'

'The Louvre is where we learn to read. But we must not be satisfied with retaining the formulas of our illustrious predecessors, let us go to study beautiful nature.'

'The sensations of colour which give light are the reasons for the abstractions which prevent me from either covering the canvas or continuing the delineation of the objects when their points of contact are fine and delicate.'

'The eye becomes concentric by looking and working. I mean to say that in an orange, an apple, a head there is a culminating point of light shade and colour, the closest to our eye. Edges of objects recede to a centre on the horizon.'

Matisse, 1869–1954. The leading painter of the school of Paris, apart from Picasso. A prolific painter of the still life, all in Matisse is colour and pleasure. His drawing is always astringent and acute. If Matisse is never intense he is never displeasing, when one sees his all too many bad imitators one realises his unique qualities. He was prolific in paint, drawings and words, some of which are quoted below:

'Don't paint the thing itself, paint the effect it produces.'

'Black is a colour – black is a force.'

'Colour exists in itself, it has its own beauty . . . I use colour as a means of expressing my emotion, and not as a transcription of nature. I use the simplest colours.'

'In still life painting consists in translating the relations of the objects of the subject by understanding the different qualities of colours and the interrelations.'

'To copy the objects in a still life is nothing, one must render the emotion they awaken. The emotion of the ensemble, the interrelation of objects, the specific character of every object modified by its relation to others all interlaced.'

Bonnard, 1867–1947. Another great painter of the school of Paris, he is the master of the still life that could equally be described as an interior. Gentle, warm and sensitive, his paintings are marvellously evocative.

'We can abstract beauty out of everything.'

'I've discovered peaches, they're so intense and soft and some of them resemble a setting sun, only it's a sunset that does not disappear conveniently enough for the painter.'

Poussin is not of course a still life painter. This Franco-Roman painter of the grand composition would probably have based a still life rather low in his canon of the painter's art, but some of his statements on painting can apply to anything. Poussin's theories, it is true, are not always his own, he quotes from the antique directly and indirectly.

'The preparation of beauty consists of three things; order, mode, and form. Order means the spacing of parts, mode has to do with quantity, species consists in line and colours.'

'Nothing is visible without light. Nothing is visible without transparent medium. Nothing is visible without boundaries. Nothing is visible without colour. Nothing is visible without distance. Nothing is visible without instrument. What comes after this cannot be learned, it pertains to the painter.'

Eugene Delacroix, 1798–1863, was the leading French

romantic painter. His work covered every branch of painting from ancient and contemporary history to still life. He was a great champion of the younger painters and in turn was a great influence on them. Delacroix passionately admired and emulated Rubens whom he called the Homer of painting.

'Once the picture has a too rough lay in, reached a condition where it is satisfying to the mind as a matter of lines, colour and effect, it is evident that if one continues to the end of work in the same manner, that is to say to proceed with sketchy painting, one loses a large part of the profit of that great simplicity of impression which one attained in the beginning.'

Odilon Redon, 1840–1916. A French symbolist painter and friend of the symbolist poets; he painted beautiful flowers, and was an influence on Gauguin. Like his painting, his writing has symbolist qualities and may lose a fair bit from being translated.

'These are, therefore, without an explanation that could be any more precise, the repercussion of a human expression placed by fantasy in an interplay of arabesques where I sincerely believe the action which will result from this in the spirit of the onlooker will inspire him to fantasies whose significance will be great or small according to his sensibility and the aptitude of his imagination to enlarge or diminish all things. Everything is derived from universal life . . . there is the world of plants, secret and normal . . . of life which the sensitive artist cannot ignore. It is nature that commands us to obey the gifts it has given us. Mine led me into dreams, I have experienced the torments of imagination and surprises it has created under my pencil, but I have conducted them and led them under those surprises according to the organic laws of art that I know. There is a kind of . . . that imagination has liberated from the care of real details to serve with freedom only for the depiction of imagined things.'

Index